THE OFFICIAL STREET FOOD COOKBOOK

THE OFFICIAL STREET FOOD COOKBOOK

BY VICTORIA ROSENTHAL

INSIGHT
EDITIONS

SAN RAFAEL · LOS ANGELES · LONDON

CONTENTS

EUROPE

ASIA

INTRODUCTION

Hello there, I'm pleased to meet you! The name's Sakura Kasugano, but you might know me as the self-taught, beautiful brawler from Tokyo! Or maybe the super helpful and hardworking arcade manager? I've been studying how to be a stronger fighter all my life, practicing moves and techniques whenever I find the time. I've even trained under Ryu, the strongest fighter out there. Well, okay, maybe not trained, per se. Sort of more like . . . emulated? Mirrored? I'm basically his protégée, even if it isn't technically official or anything.

I got stronger. I won tournaments. I came up with my own special moves. But even after all that, I don't feel stronger. Trust me, I wouldn't want to be on the other end of my Hadosho. But something just feels lacking, you know? What good is strength if it ends with me? It wasn't until I ran into Ryu outside of work one evening that I found my answer. It's not strength that lasts, but life. I realized what I wanted, but I needed some advice on how to find my place in life, so I went to the smartest person I know for some help.

Karin didn't even look up from her book when I walked in. "So, I take it Ryu caught up with you?" she asked. I was a little surprised to hear she spoke with Ryu first, but I was excited to explain my plan to her. I've met so many strong people around the world. I wanted to know what made them all wake up each day and face the challenges ahead of them. If I talked to enough martial artists and got their stories, I'd definitely find answers to my own strength. But an arcade worker's wages don't exactly cover flying around the world.

"Well, Sakura, if that's your goal, I'm entering a tournament next month," said Karin. "Why not join me?" It was the perfect plan! I'd cheer for Karin and catch up with all the fighters competing! Maybe I'd even sneak in a fight or two, but only if I had time. I ran home to start packing, but I had to make a quick stop at my favorite onigiri stall. Bouncing with excitement with my delicious rice ball in hand, I had an amazing idea.

—Sakura Kasugano

WHY STREET FOOD?

I love street food. It's the perfect representation of local culture. It's cheap and easily accessible. It's almost like street fighting in a way. People can come from all walks of life, but when we sit down on the side of the road with a basket of takoyaki or in a night market stall with some delicious som tam, we're all equal. Trends come and go, but street food builds on a long history of people perfecting their craft and making their community run. All this talk is making me hungry, and I know just what I want to do next.

If I'm going to sit down with some of the best fighters out there, I need the right approach. I have some good friends on the tournament circuit, but let's just say they aren't world-renowned for their conversation skills. Going out for some local street food would be the perfect setting to relax and get people to open up. And even better, I can eat while I'm researching! But I wonder what kind of food everyone will want?

Just like fighting, street food can be pursued in two ways: perfecting tradition and reinventing the form. Some pushcarts have been around since way before I was born, and they've never changed. It's like how Ryu and Ken are always butting heads about the proper way to use Ansatsuken. Gouken really drilled that style into their heads. Every stance must be the same, each movement rehearsed to infinity. They wake up every day and try to do the same thing even better than before.

But sometimes you've gotta throw in some new ideas and unique ingredients and get creative! I'd rather make things my own and find my own expression in a fight. Besides, I can do most of the same moves as Ryu, but I have my own flair. I didn't learn a whole lot about fighting from Dan, but I definitely saw the confidence he has in doing his own style. He doesn't get a lot of respect from other fighters, but I know he can always bounce back in his own way. And that's way more important to me than some stingy rules.

So let's do this! I'm going to travel around the world and learn what it means to be strong. And even better, I'm going to stuff my face while doing it. It would be such a waste to go on this adventure without keeping track of what I learn and what I eat, so I'll try to document my journey.

INGREDIENTS FROM AROUND THE WORLD

I know many of you reading this cookbook are just starting out in the kitchen, so don't worry if some of these recipes look a little overwhelming. I've gathered recipes from all sorts of cuisines around the world—don't be surprised if a handful of ingredients are hard to find. You may have luck scouring specialty grocery stores, international food aisles, farmers markets, or ordering online. I thought it would be helpful to describe some less-common ingredients here so you know what you're looking for. But don't fret if not everything is available! I provide some substitutions throughout this book—but to get the real flavor of these dishes, I encourage you to track these ingredients down!

AGAR-AGAR POWDER is a plant-based gelatin made from seaweed, specifically red sea algae. It's used to thicken and set liquids. It can be found in various forms including bars, flakes, and powders. For this book, I use the powder. It can be stored in the pantry for up to eight months.

AMCHUR POWDER is used in Indian cuisine. Made from unripe mangos dried in the sun and then ground into a powder, it has a tangy, sour taste very similar to dehydrated mango. It can be stored in the pantry in an airtight container for about a year.

BUBU ARARE are small baked Japanese crackers made from glutinous rice. They can be stored in the pantry in an airtight container for about three months.

CASTELVETRANO OLIVES are grown in Sicily. They're bright green with a firm texture and a rich, buttery flavor. These olives can be substituted with another firm green olive.

CHINESE FIVE-SPICE POWDER is a combination of cinnamon, Sichuan peppercorn, star anise, fennel seed, and clove. It can be stored in the pantry for up to a year, but keep in mind that spices will lose flavor the longer they are stored.

CONDENSED MILK has been gently heated, 60 percent of the water removed, mixed with sugar, and canned. This is an extremely thick, caramelized sweetened milk. It is typically found in cans that can be stored in a pantry for about a year. Once opened, it must be refrigerated and used within two weeks.

DASHI is a broth typically made from kombu and katsuoboshi. It can be made fresh or with instant powders or liquids.

DIASTATIC MALT POWDER is a grain that has been sprouted, dried, and then ground. It contains active enzymes that release sugars and help yeast grow. Adding it to dough helps improve the rise and helps achieve a golden crust.

DOUBANJIANG, sometimes sold as *la doubanjiang*, is a thick, spicy paste made from fermented broad beans, soybeans, and a variety of spices. The flavor is extremely spicy and salty. Doubanjiang can be substituted with sambal oelek or gochujang.

EVAPORATED MILK has been gently heated and 60 percent of its water removed to make a dense, creamy milk. Unlike condensed milk, it's not sweetened. It's found in cans that can be stored in a pantry for about six months. Once opened, it must be refrigerated and used within five days.

FISH SAUCE is a sweet, salty, pungent liquid made from fermented anchovies and salt. The salt content is pretty high, so the sauce can be used to replace salt in many cases and adds an extra layer of umami to boot. Be careful to not add too much because it can easily overpower a dish. Fish sauce can be stored in the pantry for two to three years.

FURIKAKE is a dried seasoning used in Japanese cuisine, on rice. It typically includes bonito flakes, seaweed, sesame seeds, sugar, and salt. It comes in a lot of different varieties like wasabi furikake and shiso furikake, so try a few to find your favorite flavor. Furikake can be stored in the pantry for one year.

GARAM MASALA is a blend of ground spices commonly found in Indian cooking.

GIARDINIERA is an Italian pickled vegetable condiment. It typically includes carrots, celery, bell peppers, and cauliflower marinated in a mixture of vinegar and olive oil. Sealed giardiniera can be stored in the pantry. Once opened, store in the refrigerator.

GLUTINOUS RICE FLOUR is ground sweet rice. Rice flour not labeled as glutinous is made from non-sweet rice. In Japanese cuisine, there are two kinds of glutinous rice flour, mochiko and shiratamako. Mochiko has the consistency of flour while shiratamako is a bunch of large coarse granules.

GOCHUJANG is a thick Korean chile paste that contains red chile peppers, sticky rice, fermented soybeans, and sweeteners. Heat levels of gochujang can vary and are displayed on the container with a spice indicator. Once gochujang is opened, it must be stored in an airtight container in the refrigerator.

HOISIN SAUCE is a sweet, thick sauce used in Chinese cuisine, especially BBQ, made from fermented soybean and Chinese five-spice powder. It can be used for cooking or just as a dipping sauce. Hoisin sauce can be stored in the pantry until opened. Once opened, store in the refrigerator.

HOJICHA is a roasted green tea from Japan. This tea is a bancha (an ordinary, everyday tea), grown out in the sun and gathered during the latter half of the harvest season. Hojicha tea has a toasty flavor profile.

HOLY BASIL is an herb used in Southeast Asian cuisine. It has a light peppery flavor with an aftertaste of clove. Holy basil can be substituted with any type of basil, although it will have a different flavor profile.

HONEYCOMB is a natural product made by honeybees. This is the housing bees use to store the honey and pollen they collect. It can be stored in the pantry in an airtight container indefinitely.

ICHIMI TOGARASHI is a single chile spice used in Japanese cuisine. Ichimi togarashi can be stored in the pantry. It can be replaced with any ground chile of your liking.

IKURA is salmon roe, typically served raw. It must be stored in the refrigerator, no longer than four days.

JAMÓN SERRANO is a salty cured ham from Spain. It can be substituted with prosciutto.

JOCHEONG is a thick, sweet syrup made from brown rice. It can be substituted with equal parts corn syrup or honey.

KASHMIRI CHILE POWDER is made from the Kashmiri chile that has been dried and ground. The Kashmiri chile has mild heat with a vibrant red coloring. A good substitute for Kashmiri chile powder includes paprika or another mild chile.

KIMCHI is a spicy Korean fermented vegetable dish. Napa cabbage is the most common vegetable used for kimchi. It is prepared with a brine and spices, similar to a pickling process. Kimchi goes beyond that and allows the vegetables to ferment. Kimchi must be stored in the refrigerator and occasionally opened to allow pressure from the fermentation to release.

KOSHIAN is a fine, smooth red bean paste used in Japanese cuisine. When opened, it can be stored in an airtight container in the refrigerator up to two weeks.

LINGUICA is a Portuguese pork sausage seasoned with garlic and paprika. It can be substituted with another smoky garlic sausage like andouille or kielbasa.

MANCHEGO is a Spanish aged, semi-hard cheese made from sheep's milk. It's commonly wrapped in an inedible rind. The cheese has a mild, creamy, earthy flavor and can be substituted with Pecorino Romano or Monterey Jack.

MISO is a Japanese paste made from fermented soybeans. Miso comes in several varieties including white (the mildest) and red (allowed to age longer, making it saltier, with a stronger flavor). Miso can be stored in an airtight container in the refrigerator.

MORTADELLA is an Italian smoked sausage made from pork, and it often contains pork fat cubes and pistachios.

NORI is a dried sheet of edible seaweed used in Japanese cuisine. Its most popular use is to wrap sushi rolls. Nori can be stored in a cool pantry.

OYSTER SAUCE is a thick sauce made from oysters used in Chinese cuisine. It is savory with a slight hint of sweetness. Even though the sauce is made from oysters, the fishy flavor is mild, while the caramelized flavor stands out.

PAIO is a Portuguese pork sausage seasoned with garlic and peppers. It can be substituted with chorizo.

PALM SUGAR is a sweetener made from nectar of the coconut flowers or palm flowers. Palm sugar can be substituted with brown sugar.

PLANTAINS are related to bananas but are much starchier and can't be eaten raw. Unripe plantains will be green in color. As they ripen, their skin turns yellow (medium) and eventually black (fully ripe).

PRICKLY PEAR is the fruit of the nopal cactus. These fruits can range from green (less sweet variety) to red (sweeter).

RICE PAPER is a super-thin wrapper made from rice used in Vietnamese cuisine. The sheets are dry and need to be rehydrated before use.

SAUERKRAUT is pickled and fermented cabbage, popular in Eastern European cuisine.

SHAOXING WINE is a rice wine used in Chinese cuisine. It can be stored in a cool pantry for about six months.

SICHUAN PEPPERCORNS are a reddish spice, similar in size to black peppercorn, grown in China. These peppercorns give your mouth a unique numbing sensation. They can be stored in the pantry.

SUI MI YA CAI is preserved mustard greens used in Sichuanese cuisine. It can be stored in the pantry. Once opened, it must be stored in the refrigerator in an airtight container for about two months.

TAHINI are a paste made from ground white sesame seeds and oil. Store-bought tahini can be stored in the pantry for up to six months.

TAMARIND JUICE is made from tamarind pods. Inside the pod is a very sticky, tart, sweet fruit. Tamarind juice can be substituted with equal parts lime juice and brown sugar.

TAPIOCA PEARLS are small spheres made from the extracted starch of cassava. When cooked, they are very chewy.

THAI BASIL is an herb with purple stems and green leaves used in Southeast Asian cuisine. It has a mildly spicy licorice-like flavor. It is a slightly sturdier herb than Italian basil and is more stable at high cooking temperatures. Thai basil can be substituted with any type of basil, but it will have a different flavor profile.

TONKATSU SAUCE is a thick, sweet sauce used in Japanese cuisine. It can be stored in the pantry. Once opened, it can be stored in the refrigerator in an airtight container for about two months.

VITAL WHEAT GLUTEN is wheat flour that has had most of its starch removed, leaving the wheat proteins behind. The protein content is between 75 and 85 percent. Adding it to a dough will yield a much more elastic and chewy texture.

WASABI is the stem of the *Wasabia japonica* plant, found in Japan. Authentic wasabi must be grated and served immediately to avoid losing its flavor and has a shelf life of one to two days at room temperature and one month in the refrigerator. More common is a wasabi substitute made of horseradish, mustard powder, and food coloring. This substitute is spicier and more pungent but can be stored in the refrigerator for up to one year.

YUZU is a sour and tart citrus grown primarily in East Asia. Typically used for juice and zest, one fresh yuzu can yield two to three teaspoons of juice. It might be difficult to find fresh yuzu, but juice and frozen zest can be easier to locate. Yuzu can be substituted with another citrus of your choice, such as a combination of lime and orange.

DIETARY NOTES

ALLERGY NOTES

It took a lot of training and creativity to figure out my own fighting style, so likewise don't be afraid of changing the recipe to your own liking. If you've got dietary restrictions or just want to try a creative spin on a dish, feel free to try substitutions to fit your needs.

ADAPTING TO VEGETARIAN DIETS

Several recipes in this book are vegetarian or vegan friendly. Many other recipes can be adapted to your dietary needs. Replace meat broths and stocks with vegetable broths and stocks. Swap out proteins with your favorite grilled vegetable or meat substitute. This will affect cooking times, so plan ahead.

ADAPTING TO GLUTEN-FREE DIETS

For most recipes, you can use equal ratios of gluten substitute for flour, but be prepared to modify the quantity in case the consistency seems off compared to how the dish is described in the recipe.

ADAPTING TO LACTOSE-FREE DIETS

Feel free to replace milk and heavy cream with your favorite non-dairy milk. There are also plenty of butter alternatives available that are really great options. I don't suggest replacing butter with oil, because it doesn't give the consistency needed for certain recipes. If you do use oil, approach it in small batches.

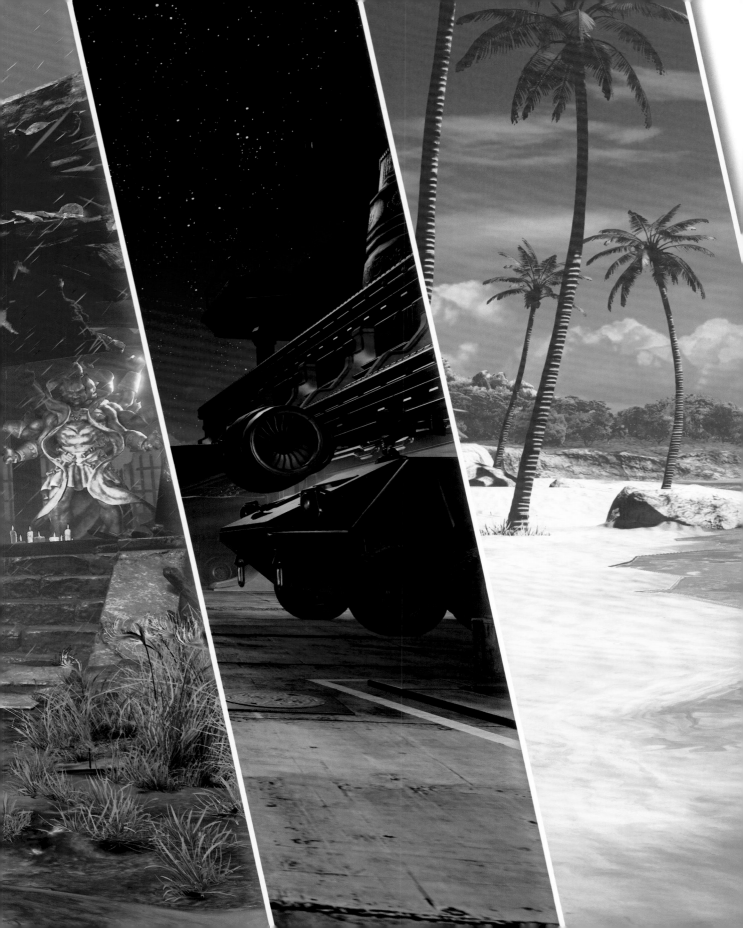

BASICS

Before we get started on our trip around the world, I thought it would be helpful to share a few basic recipes that are perfect to have in your culinary arsenal!

BURGER BUNS

These are light, fluffy, and perfect for burgers. But, honestly, you can use 'em with any kind of sandwich. The black and white sesame seeds add flair on top.

DIFFICULTY: ▬ ▬ ▬ ▭ ▭ ▭ ▭
PREP TIME: 1 HOUR
REST TIME: 2 HOURS
COOK TIME: 20 MINUTES
YIELD: 6 BUNS
DIETARY NOTES: DAIRY, VEGETARIAN
USED IN: SMASH BURGERS (PAGE 65)

FOR THE TANGZHONG:

3 tablespoons (27 g) bread flour
⅓ cup (79 ml) milk

FOR THE DOUGH:

1 tablespoon (12 g) active dry yeast
⅔ cup (158 ml) warm milk, roughly
   100°F to 110°F (37°C to 43°C), plus
   more if needed
2½ cups (410 g) bread flour, plus
   more if needed
½ tablespoon (6 g) salt
1 teaspoon (4 g) garlic powder
½ teaspoon (2 g) onion powder
1 tablespoon (16 g) granulated sugar
1 large egg
3 tablespoons (42 g) unsalted butter,
   softened
Neutral oil or nonstick spray, for
   oiling

FOR THE EGG WASH:

1 egg
2 tablespoons (30 ml) milk

FOR THE TOPPING:

2 teaspoons (6 g) black sesame seeds
1 teaspoon (3 g) white sesame seeds

TO MAKE THE TANGZHONG:

Combine bread flour and milk in a saucepan. Heat over medium-high heat and whisk until it comes together, about one minute. Set aside and allow to cool.

TO MAKE THE DOUGH:

Combine yeast and milk in a small bowl, and let rest for 5 minutes, allowing the yeast to become active. In a large bowl of a stand mixer, combine the bread flour, salt, garlic powder, onion powder, and sugar. Add the tangzhong, milk, and egg to the bowl, and mix until it just comes together.

While the dough begins to knead, add the butter 1 tablespoon (14 g) at a time. Knead the dough for 5 minutes. If the dough is too sticky, add 1 tablespoon of flour at a time. If it is too dry, add 1 tablespoon of milk at a time. Lightly oil a large bowl with a neutral oil such as canola or nonstick spray. Transfer dough to the oiled bowl, cover, and let rest in a warm location for 1 hour or until it has doubled in size.

Once doubled, punch down and knead. Line a baking sheet with parchment paper. Divide the dough into 6 equal portions. Shape into balls, place on the baking sheet, and lightly press down slightly to widen. Cover with plastic wrap, and let rest for 30 to 60 minutes, or until doubled in size.

Preheat oven to 375°F (190°C).

TO MAKE THE EGG WASH:

Whisk an egg and 2 tablespoons of milk in a small bowl. Remove the plastic wrap from the baking sheet, and brush each of the buns with egg wash. Combine the sesame seeds in a small bowl. Sprinkle the sesame seeds on the each of the buns. Bake for 16 to 19 minutes or until golden brown.

Tangzhong is a paste used to improve the texture of bread, making it soft and fluffy.

JAPANESE MILK BREAD

This is a much sweeter loaf of bread than your usual kind. If you can't finish it before it starts getting stale, it makes for a wonderful French toast!

DIFFICULTY: ▬▬▬ ▬▬ ▬▬ ▬▬ ▬▬

PREP TIME: 1 HOUR

REST TIME: 2 HOURS

COOK TIME: 30 TO 45 MINUTES

YIELD: 1 LOAF

DIETARY NOTES: DAIRY, VEGETARIAN

USED IN: FRUIT SANDO (PAGE 123)

FOR THE TANGZHONG:

2 tablespoons (25 g) bread flour

⅓ cup (79 ml) milk

FOR THE DOUGH:

1 tablespoon (12 g) active dry yeast

¾ cup (177 ml) milk, warm, plus more if needed

2¾ cup (410 g) bread flour, plus more if needed

1 teaspoon (3 g) salt

1 teaspoon (3 g) ground cardamom

½ teaspoon (1.5 g) ground cinnamon

⅓ cup (67 g) sugar

1 egg, room temperature

¼ cup (56 g) unsalted butter, softened

Neutral oil such as canola or nonstick spray, for oiling

FOR THE EGG WASH:

1 egg

2 tablespoons (30 ml) milk

TO MAKE THE TANGZHONG:

Combine bread flour and milk in a small saucepan over medium-high heat. Whisk until it comes together, about 1 minute. Set aside to cool.

TO MAKE THE DOUGH:

Combine yeast and milk in a small bowl, and let rest for 5 minutes, allowing the yeast to become active and frothy. In a large bowl of a stand mixer fitted with the dough-hook attachment, combine the bread flour, salt, cardamom, cinnamon, and sugar. Add the tangzhong, yeast mixture, and egg to the bowl, and mix until it just comes together.

While the dough begins to form, add the butter 1 tablespoon (14 g) at a time. Knead the dough for 5 minutes. If the dough is too sticky, add 1 tablespoon (8 g) of flour at a time. If it is too dry, add 1 tablespoon of milk at a time. Lightly oil a large bowl with a neutral oil or nonstick spray. Transfer to an oiled bowl, cover, and let rest in a warm location for 1 hour or until it has doubled in size.

Punch down the dough, and knead for a few minutes. Divide the dough into 3 equal portions. Grease a deep loaf pan or other deep bread-baking pan. Take one of the portions and roll the dough out into a long rectangle. Make sure the width of the rolled-out portion is not wider than the baking dish you are using. Starting from a short end of the rectangle, carefully roll up the dough. Place in the prepared baking pan, seam-side down. Repeat with the other portions. Cover with plastic wrap, and allow to rise again at room temperature for 30 minutes or until it doubles in size.

Preheat oven to 350°F (180°C).

TO MAKE THE EGG WASH:

In a small bowl, whisk the egg and milk to combine. Remove the plastic wrap from the baking pan, and brush the top of the bread with the egg wash. Bake for 30 minutes or until golden brown and cooked through.

LADI PAV

I hadn't tried this bread before my trip, but it's a delicious way to scoop up every last bite. I'll definitely be making a full batch for myself.

DIFFICULTY: ▬▬ ▬▬ ▬▬ ▬▬ ▬▬
PREP TIME: 1 HOUR
REST TIME: 2 HOURS
COOK TIME: 20 MINUTES
YIELD: 12 BUNS
DIETARY NOTES: DAIRY, VEGETARIAN
USED IN: PAV BHAJI (PAGE 139)

INGREDIENTS:

1½ cups (355 ml) milk, divided, plus more for dough
2 tablespoons (26 g) sugar
2¼ teaspoons (8 g) active dry yeast
3 cups (409 g) all-purpose flour, plus more if needed
1 teaspoon (4 g) baking powder
2 teaspoons (7 g) salt
2 tablespoons (13 g) milk powder
¼ cup (56 g) unsalted butter, plus more for pan
Neutral oil or nonstick spray, for oiling

INSTRUCTIONS:

Combine ½ cup milk and the sugar in a small saucepan. Heat until the sugar dissolves. Allow to cool to 105°F to 110°F (41°C to 43°C). Whisk in the yeast, and let rest for 5 minutes, allowing the yeast to become active and frothy.

Combine flour, baking powder, salt, and milk powder in a large bowl. Add the yeast mixture, and mix until it just comes together. Add the remaining cup of milk in slowly, ¼ cup (59 ml) at a time, until the dough comes together.

Add the butter 1 tablespoon (14 g) at a time. Knead the dough for 5 minutes. If the dough is too sticky, add 1 tablespoon (8 g) of flour at a time. If it is too dry, add 1 tablespoon (15 g) of milk at a time. Lightly oil a large bowl with a neutral oil or nonstick spray. Shape the dough into a ball, place in the oiled bowl, and cover. Let rest at room temperature until the dough doubles in size, 1 to 2 hours.

Prepare a 13-by-15-inch (33-by-38-cm) deep baking pan with butter. Punch down the dough and knead. Split the dough into 12 equal portions. Shape into balls, and arrange in the prepared baking pan. The balls should be about 1 inch apart. Cover with a kitchen towel, and let rest at room temperature for 30 to 60 minutes or until doubled in size.

Preheat oven to 400°F (205°C). Brush the now-adjacent buns with milk. Bake for 12 to 18 minutes or until golden brown. Allow to cool for 5 minutes. Remove from the pan, and allow to cool completely on a metal rack.

MUFFULETTA BREAD

I love using this bread for a lot of different sandwiches! It also works really well as a base for garlic bread.

DIFFICULTY: ▬▬ ▬▬ ▬▬ ▬▬ ▬▬

PREP TIME: 1 HOUR

REST TIME: 2 HOURS

COOK TIME: 20 TO 30 MINUTES

YIELD: 1 LOAF

DIETARY NOTES: DAIRY, VEGETARIAN

USED IN: PRESSED MUFFULETTA (PAGE 41)

INGREDIENTS:

- 1 cup (237 ml) warm water, 105°F to 110°F (40°C to 43°C), plus 2 tablespoons (30 ml) cold water
- 2 tablespoons (30 ml) olive oil, plus more for bowl
- 2¼ teaspoons (8 g) active dry yeast
- 3 cups (522 g) bread flour
- 1½ tablespoons (19 g) sugar
- 1 teaspoon (4 g) vital wheat gluten
- 2 teaspoons (8 g) salt
- 2 tablespoons (28 g) unsalted butter
- 1 egg
- ½ tablespoon (8 g) sesame seeds

INSTRUCTIONS:

Combine the warm water, olive oil, and yeast in a large bowl, then set aside for a few minutes to activate the yeast. Meanwhile, combine the bread flour, sugar, vital wheat gluten, and salt in a medium bowl. Add the dry ingredients to the large bowl. Mix until it just comes together. Add the butter, and continue to mix until blended.

Transfer to a floured work surface, and knead for about 10 minutes. Shape into a ball, place in an oiled bowl, and cover. Let rest at room temperature until the dough doubles in size, 1 to 2 hours.

Punch the dough, and roll it out to a flat, round disc roughly 10 inches (25 cm) across. Place on a baking sheet lined with parchment paper. Cover, and let rise at room temperature for another hour.

Preheat oven to 425°F (220°C). Whisk an egg with the cold water, and brush the top of the dough. Sprinkle with sesame seeds. Bake for 8 minutes. Reduce the heat to 375°F (190°C), and bake for another 20 to 25 minutes, until golden brown.

SUSHI RICE

Rice is one of my favorite ingredients, but sushi rice takes this simple ingredient to a whole new level! It's amazing on its own, and it goes great with most meals.

DIFFICULTY: ▬▬ ▬▬ ▬▬ ▬▬ ▬▬

PREP TIME: 30 MINUTES

COOK TIME: 45 MINUTES

YIELD: 3 CUPS COOKED RICE

DIETARY NOTES: VEGAN

USED IN: CHIRASHI (PAGE 165), ONIGIRI (PAGE 191, 193)

INGREDIENTS:

3 cups (424 g) sushi rice

Water (follow your rice cooker's directions)

3 tablespoons (45 ml) rice vinegar

2 tablespoons (26 g) sugar

½ teaspoon (2 g) salt

INSTRUCTIONS:

Put rice in a large bowl, and fill it up with cold water. With your hands, rub in a circular motion. The water will become cloudy, which means it needs to be rinsed. Strain out the water, and repeat until the water runs clear.

Place the cleaned rice and amount of water indicated into your rice cooker, and allow the rice to cook. When the rice is done, remove from the rice cooker, and place in a large non-metallic bowl.

In a small bowl, combine rice vinegar, sugar, and salt. Use a rice paddle to fold in the vinegar mixture to the rice while the rice is still hot. Continue to gently fold and turn the rice until it has cooled down.

PAV BHAJI MASALA

This spice blend can be found pre-mixed in Indian grocery stores, but you can create your own. Trust me, once you make the Pav Bhaji (page 139) curry, you're going to want a lot of this spice mix around to make it over and over again!

DIFFICULTY: ▬▬ ▬▬ ▬▬ ▬▬ ▬▬

PREP TIME: 10 MINUTES

YIELD: ½ CUP

DIETARY NOTES: VEGAN

USED IN: PAV BHAJI (PAGE 139)

INGREDIENTS:

1 black cardamom pod

1½ tablespoons (7 g) coriander seeds

2 whole cloves

½ cinnamon stick

1 teaspoon (3 g) black peppercorns

1 teaspoon (2 g) fennel seeds

3 to 4 tablespoons (36 to 48 g) Kashmiri chile powder

2 teaspoons (7 g) amchur powder

1 tablespoon (10 g) ground cumin

INSTRUCTIONS:

Place the cardamom, coriander seeds, cloves, cinnamon stick, peppercorns, and fennel seeds in a small saucepan over medium heat, and toast the spices until they become fragrant, about 5 minutes. Shake the pan frequently to prevent the spices from burning.

Remove from the heat, and allow to cool. Transfer to a spice grinder or mortar and pestle, and blend until finely ground. Place in a bowl, and combine with the Kashmiri chile powder, amchur powder, and cumin. Move to an airtight container. Can be stored for up to two months.

PICKLED RED ONION

Want to take your red onions to the next level? Pickling them will cut the bitterness and add great flavor. Anytime a recipe calls for raw red onions, I'll pickle them!

DIFFICULTY: ▬▬ ▬ ▬ ▬ ▬

PREP TIME: 30 MINUTES

YIELD: 1 CUP

DIETARY NOTES: VEGAN

USED IN: CARNE ASADA TORTAS (PAGE 51), CARNITAS (PAGE 69), BACON SANDWICH (PAGE 37)

INGREDIENTS:

¾ cup (177 ml) warm water

½ cup (118 ml) rice vinegar, plus more if needed

1 tablespoon (13 g) sugar

½ tablespoon (6 g) salt

10 black peppercorns

1 rosemary sprig

1 medium red onion, sliced

INSTRUCTIONS:

Combine the warm water, rice vinegar, sugar, and salt in a large container with an airtight lid. Whisk together until the sugar has dissolved. Add the peppercorns, rosemary sprig, and red onion. If the red onions are not covered, add more rice vinegar. Cover, and refrigerate for at least 30 minutes. The longer it is left to pickle, the more flavorful the red onion will become. Remove the rosemary sprig after 1 week. Store in the refrigerator for up to 2 weeks.

MANGO CHUTNEY

This delicious sauce is extremely popular in India but deserves to be famous all around the world! It can be paired with rice, breads, and so much more. This chutney features mango, but there are many different types you should try if you get a chance!

DIFFICULTY: ▬▬ ▬ ▬ ▬ ▬

PREP TIME: 50 MINUTES

YIELD: 2 CUPS

DIETARY NOTES: VEGAN

USED IN: CHICKEN MASALA ROTI WRAP (PAGE 99)

INGREDIENTS:

½ cinnamon stick

1 teaspoon (3 g) cumin seeds

½ teaspoon (1 g) coriander seeds

1 whole clove

1 star anise

3 green cardamom pods

2 large mangoes, peeled and cut into chunks

2-inch (5-cm) piece fresh ginger, peeled and grated

1 teaspoon (1 g) red chile flakes

¼ cup (50 g) sugar

½ cup (130 g) brown sugar

2 tablespoons (30 ml) water

1 tablespoon (15 ml) white vinegar

½ teaspoon (2.5 g) salt

INSTRUCTIONS:

Place the cinnamon stick, cumin seeds, coriander seeds, clove, star anise, and cardamom in a cheesecloth. Place the rest of the ingredients in a medium saucepan over medium-high heat, and bring to a boil.

Reduce the heat, and simmer for 25 minutes. Add the cheesecloth with spices, and simmer for an additional 15 minutes, or until the mango is soft enough to mash.

Discard the cheesecloth of spices, transfer the chutney to a container that has an airtight lid, and allow to cool completely. Once cooled, seal and refrigerate for up to a week.

TZATZIKI

This is a great sauce to pair with Greek recipes, but it's so delicious and versatile that I sometimes sneak some onto other things as well.

DIFFICULTY:

PREP TIME: 20 MINUTES

YIELD: 2 CUPS

DIETARY NOTES: DAIRY, VEGETARIAN

USED IN: SOUVLAKI (PAGE 109)

INGREDIENTS:

1 seedless cucumber, peeled and grated

2 (2 g) garlic cloves, minced

1½ cups (427 g) greek yogurt

2 tablespoon (30 ml) olive oil

½ tablespoon (7.5 ml) red wine vinegar

Zest and juice of 1 lemon

1 teaspoon (1 g) dill

1 teaspoon (1 g) oregano

½ teaspoon (1 g) salt

INSTRUCTIONS:

Salt the cucumber in a strainer placed over a bowl and let sit for about 10 minutes to drain.

In a bowl, mix together all of the other ingredients.

After the cucumber has drained squeeze out the extra liquid with your hands or in a cheesecloth. Add to the other ingredients and mix together. Can be stored in the refrigerator for a week.

CUCUMBER RAITA

Whew! I found tons of delicious spicy foods in India, but if the heat ever became too much for me, all it would take is a spoonful of raita with my food to cool me down so I could keep eating!

DIFFICULTY:

PREP TIME: 5 MINUTES

YIELD: 2 CUPS

DIETARY NOTES: DAIRY, VEGETARIAN

USED IN: CHICKEN MASALA ROTI WRAP (PAGE 99)

INGREDIENTS:

1 cup (225 g) plain yogurt

½ cup (118 ml) water

½ teaspoon (2.5 g) salt

½ teaspoon (2 g) sugar

1 cucumber, peeled and grated

2 tablespoons (5 g) fresh cilantro, chopped

2 teaspoons (4 g) ground coriander

1 teaspoon (2 g) ground cumin

INSTRUCTIONS:

Combine all the ingredients in a container that has an airtight lid. Whisk together, and season with additional salt to your liking. Seal and refrigerate for up to a week.

NORTH AMERICA

DIFFICULTY:

PREP TIME: 1 HOUR

REST TIME: 2 TO 3 HOURS

YIELD: 16 PIECES

DIETARY NOTES: DAIRY, VEGETARIAN

NANAIMO BARS

While exploring the streets of Metro City with Cody, I was surprised to see a mountain lumbering in the distance. "That's Abigail," Cody grunted. "Sakura, make sure you never find yourself in a fight with him. He's nothing but trouble. But I can't stop taking my ride to his shop when it breaks down—the nanaimo bars they make there are worth the headache."

FOR THE BOTTOM LAYER:

2 cups (175 g) graham crackers, crumbled

½ cup (55 g) walnuts, coarsely chopped

¾ cup (43 g) unsweetened coconut flakes

½ cup (112 g) unsalted butter

¼ cup (38 g) plus 1 tablespoon (7.5 g) cocoa powder

3 tablespoons (39 g) sugar

1 tablespoon (14 g) brown sugar

1 egg, room temperature

1 teaspoon (5 ml) vanilla extract

1 teaspoon (3 g) salt

FOR THE MIDDLE LAYER:

¼ cup (54 g) unsalted butter, room temperature

2 cups (265 g) confectioners' sugar

2 tablespoons (18 g) cornstarch

½ teaspoon (1.5 g) salt

1 tablespoon (15 ml) vanilla extract

Seeds of ½ vanilla bean

2 to 3 tablespoons (30 to 45 ml) heavy cream

FOR THE TOP LAYER:

4 ounces (113 g) dark chocolate, coarsely chopped

1 tablespoon (22 g) unsalted butter

1 teaspoon (3 g) salt

TO MAKE THE BOTTOM LAYER:

Combine the crumbled graham crackers, walnuts, and coconut flakes in a large bowl.

Heat the butter in a medium saucepan over medium heat until just melted. Remove from the heat, and whisk in cocoa powder and sugars.

Whisk the egg in a small bowl. Slowly pour the egg into the saucepan while whisking vigorously. Once combined, return the saucepan to the stove over low heat. Keep whisking, and cook until slightly thickened, 1 to 2 minutes. Remove from the heat, and add vanilla extract and salt. Pour into the bowl with the graham cracker mixture. Mix together well.

Line an 8-inch (20-cm) square baking pan with aluminum foil to ease removal after baking. Transfer the mixture to the baking pan, and press into an even layer. Refrigerate for 1 hour.

TO MAKE THE MIDDLE LAYER:

Whisk butter until smooth. Add the confectioners' sugar, cornstarch, salt, vanilla extract, and vanilla bean seeds. Whisk until smooth. Add heavy cream 1 tablespoon at a time to slightly loosen, making sure it is thick but thin enough to spread. Spread over the bottom layer evenly. Refrigerate for at least 1 hour.

TO MAKE THE TOP LAYER:

Place the chocolate and the butter in a heatproof bowl. Pour about 1 inch of water in a saucepan, and bring to a simmer over medium-high heat. Place the bowl on top, and mix the chocolate until it melts. Remove from the heat. Whisk in the salt, and let cool slightly, about 5 minutes. Pour over the middle layer, and refrigerate for 10 to 15 minutes, until the chocolate has just set. Cut into 16 pieces. Store in the refrigerator for up to 2 weeks.

How does Abigail make such delicate, even layers with the same hands that can bend metal?

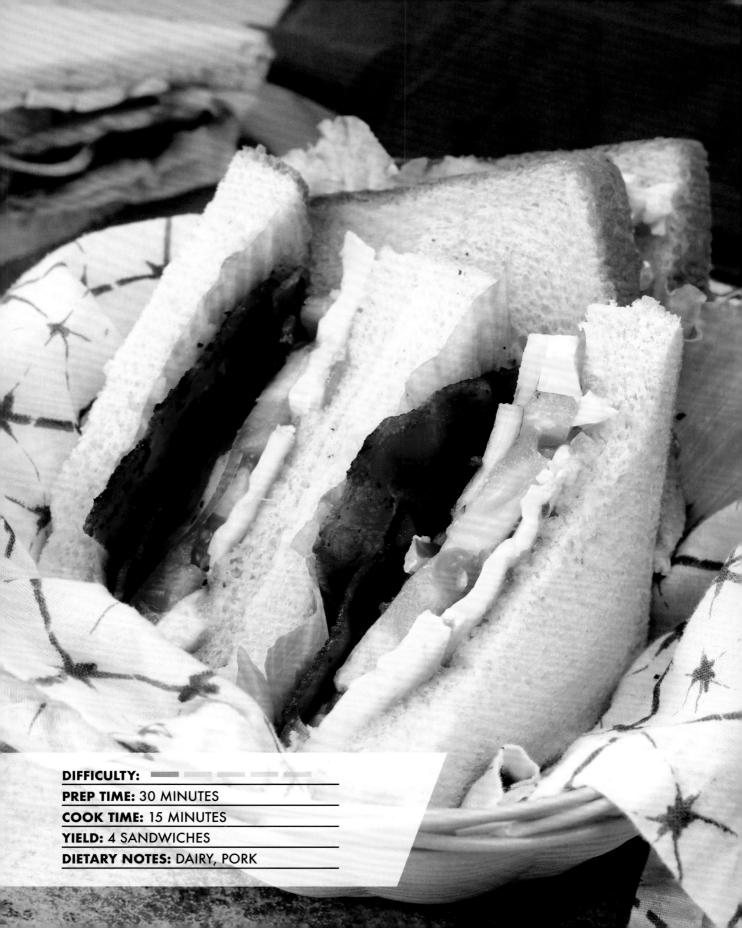

DIFFICULTY: ▬▬ ▬ ▬ ▬ ▬
PREP TIME: 30 MINUTES
COOK TIME: 15 MINUTES
YIELD: 4 SANDWICHES
DIETARY NOTES: DAIRY, PORK

BACON SANDWICH

I grabbed a bite with Alex when I visited New York, hoping to get some advice, but I'm so grateful that his friend Patricia joined us. He barely said a word while Patricia and I talked for hours about anything and everything. Alex was just happy to get out and enjoy a bacon sandwich, but I could definitely see between bites that he really cared for her. She's clearly the reason he continues to train and get stronger.

INGREDIENTS:

8 slices Texas toast or sliced white
   bread
Fig jam, store bought
Brie
4 thick tomato slices
Pickled Red Onion (page 29)
12 bacon slices, cooked
4 lettuce leaves

INSTRUCTIONS:

Spread a thin layer of fig jam on each slice of bread. Top 4 of the slices with brie, tomato, Pickled Red Onion, bacon, and lettuce. Top each sandwich with the other slice of bread. Cut into triangle portions.

DIFFICULTY:

PREP TIME: 15 MINUTES

YIELD: 1 DRINK

DIETARY NOTES: VEGAN

CHARGING BUFFALO

Chun-Li called me looking to blow off some steam, so I grabbed some drinks with her. She had been trying to track down the Shadaloo executive and former boxer, Balrog, but her last lead went nowhere. Chun-Li ordered an old-fashioned, telling me she kept drinking them on her investigation, thinking Balrog's favorite drink would put her in his mindset.

INGREDIENTS:

6 mint leaves, plus more for garnish

4 cherries, pitted and halved, plus more for garnish

¼ lemon

1 ounce (30 ml) tart cherry juice

½ ounce (15 ml) simple syrup

2 ounces (60 ml) bourbon

1 ounce (30 ml) Luxardo

Large ice cubes

INSTRUCTIONS:

Muddle the mint, cherries, and lemon in a cocktail shaker. Add the cherry juice, simple syrup, bourbon, Luxardo, and ice. Cover and shake for 10 seconds.

Prepare a glass with a large ice cube, extra mint, and cherries. Pour the mixed drink through a mesh strainer into the glass.

DIFFICULTY: ▬ ▬ ▬ ▬ ▬ ▬

PREP TIME: 1 HOUR

REST TIME: AT LEAST 48 HOURS

COOK TIME: 1 HOUR

YIELD: 4 TO 8 PORTIONS

DIETARY NOTES: DAIRY, PORK

PRESSED MUFFULETTA

I was worried that Charlie's unnatural reappearance was weighing heavily on Guile's mind, but he was happy to sit down and enjoy one of Charlie's favorite meals while reminiscing about their Air Force days. I could see some pain in his eyes when he was telling old stories of the trouble they got into, but I think he's found a way to turn that into strength without letting it get twisted into vengeance.

FOR THE OLIVE SALAD:

1¼ cups (190 g) pitted green olives

¾ cup (70 g) Castelvetrano olives, or other firm green olive

½ cup (85 g) kalamata olives

½ cup (100 g) roasted red peppers

1 cup (200 g) giardiniera

5 garlic cloves, minced

2 tablespoons (17 g) capers

1½ tablespoons (2 g) oregano

½ cup (100 g) olive oil

2 tablespoons (15 ml) red wine vinegar

Salt and black pepper

FOR THE SANDWICH:

1 Muffuletta Bread (page 25)

3 tablespoons (45 ml) olive oil

4 garlic cloves, grated

6 slices (160 g) ham

10 slices (200 g) mozzarella

10 slices (140 g) mortadella

20 slices (100 g) salami

8 slices (156 g) provolone

6 slices (85 g) prosciutto

TO MAKE THE OLIVE SALAD:

Finely chop the olives, vegetables and garlic and combine in a bowl with the rest of the ingredients. Season with salt and pepper to taste. Cover and let rest in the refrigerator for at least 2 days. Afterward, the olive salad can be stored in the refrigerator for up to 3 weeks.

TO MAKE THE SANDWICH:

Cut Muffuletta Bread in half crosswise. Whisk together olive oil and grated garlic cloves in a small bowl. Brush the garlic olive oil on the inside parts of each bread slice.

Take the bottom of the loaf, place a thick layer of olive salad and lightly press the salad into the bread. Add a layer of ham, then a layer of mozzarella. Add a layer of mortadella and salami, then a layer of provolone, and then the prosciutto. Finally, add a thin layer of olive salad and top with the loaf top.

Tightly wrap the sandwich in plastic wrap. Place in the refrigerator with a bit of weight on top of it for at least 1 hour. Flip the sandwich and place the weight back on. Let rest for 1 more hour. Take out and cut into quarters, then serve and enjoy!

This makes just enough for about two thin layers in the muffuletta. Double it if you want thicker layers of olive goodness!

DIFFICULTY: ▬ ▬ ▬ ▬ ▬ ▬

PREP TIME: 20 MINUTES

COOK TIME: 30 MINUTES

YIELD: 1 DRINK

DIETARY NOTES: GLUTEN-FREE, VEGETARIAN

SONIC BOOM

Since Charlie was such a scotch enthusiast, Guile used to mix this drink to pester him. Scotch is supposed to be enjoyed straight, but this cocktail is tasty enough to be an exception to the rule. Now, Guile makes it in his memory, wishing Charlie were still around to raise objections. At least that's what Guile's expression told me. He mostly just stared at his glass.

FOR THE HONEY GINGER SYRUP:

½ cup (135 g) honey
¼ cup (50 g) sugar
½ cup (118 ml) water
2-inch (5-cm) piece fresh ginger,
    peeled and sliced

FOR THE ASSEMBLY:

Ice
3 ounces (90 ml) scotch
1 ounce (30 ml) lemon juice
1 ounce (30 ml) Honey Ginger Syrup
1 ounce (30 ml) Islay scotch (optional)
Candied ginger, for garnish

TO MAKE THE HONEY GINGER SYRUP:

Combine honey, sugar, water, and ginger in a small saucepan over medium-high heat. Whisk until the sugar has dissolved. Bring to a boil, then reduce the heat, and simmer for 20 minutes. Remove from the heat, and strain into an airtight container. Allow to cool.

Once the syrup is cooled, you can make the drinks immediately, but I recommend covering the syrup and allowing the flavors to meld in the refrigerator for at least 12 hours. Syrup can be kept for up to 2 weeks.

TO ASSEMBLE THE DRINK:

Fill a cocktail shaker with ice, and add scotch, lemon juice, and honey ginger syrup. Cover and shake for 10 seconds. Pour the mixture from the shaker (do not include the ice) into a chilled glass with fresh large ice.

Top with the Islay scotch if using, and garnish with candied ginger.

DIFFICULTY: ▬ ▬ ▬ ▬ ▭ ▭ ▭

PREP TIME: 30 MINUTES

COOK TIME: 20 MINUTES

REST TIME: 30 MINUTES

YIELD: 4 SANDWICHES

DIETARY NOTES: DAIRY

CHEESESTEAK

I told Cody I wanted to try the street food he thinks best represents the city. He immediately knew where to go, motioning me to follow and declaring, "Three blocks that way, the best street meat in town. My treat!" He wasn't wrong, either. The cheese and meat together with the onions were absolutely delicious. I could honestly eat these cheesesteaks every day if I lived here.

INGREDIENTS:

1 ½ pounds (680 g) rib eye

3 teaspoons (44 ml) canola oil, divided

1 medium yellow onion, diced

Salt

Black pepper

Garlic powder

12 slices white American cheese

8 slices white provolone

4 French rolls, split lengthwise

INSTRUCTIONS:

Freeze the rib eye for 30 minutes so it's easy to cut. Slice the beef as thin as possible, and then roughly chop.

Heat a cast iron pan on high. Add oil, and once heated, add the onion, and cook until golden brown, 8 to 10 minutes. Transfer to a plate.

Add an additional teaspoon of canola oil to the cast iron pan. Place a fourth of the steak in the pan, and chop additionally with a metal spatula. Cook until the meat starts to crisp up, 2 to 3 minutes.

Add a fourth of the cooked onion then add salt, black pepper, and garlic powder to taste. Mix together well. Top with 2 slices of provolone and 3 slices of American cheese. Cover with a lid, and cook until the cheese begins to melt.

Place a French roll cut-side down on top of the meat, and cover again and cook for another 2 minutes. Carefully pick up the sandwich with the spatula, and flip the sandwich bread-side-down on the plate, then fold the sandwich to serve. Repeat with the remaining meat and toppings to make 4 sandwiches.

DIFFICULTY: ▬▬

PREP TIME: 15 MINUTES

YIELD: 2 DRINKS

DIETARY NOTES: DAIRY, GLUTEN-FREE,
PEANUTS, VEGETARIAN

TORNADO SWEEP

I still can't get used to seeing Cody out free on the streets, let alone as the mayor of Metro City. I asked him how he handles people's perceptions of him. "Honestly, Sakura, nothing's really changed," he said with a smirk as he handed me a delicious-looking milkshake from his favorite stop. "I always tried to do right by Metro City. Now I get free rein to do it out in the open."

INGREDIENTS:

1 banana
⅓ cup (85 g) peanut butter
¼ teaspoon (1 ml) almond extract
¼ cup (59 ml) milk, plus more if
    needed
350 g vanilla ice cream, plus more
    if needed
Chocolate sauce, for topping
Whipped cream, for topping

INSTRUCTIONS:

Place the banana, peanut butter, almond extract, and milk in a blender. Blend until smooth. Add the vanilla ice cream, and blend. If the mixture is too thick, add additional milk. If it is too thin, add extra ice cream.

Drizzle a few lines of chocolate sauce in a cup. Pour in the milkshake, and top with whipped cream.

DIFFICULTY: ▬▬ ▬ ▬

PREP TIME: 1 HOUR

COOK TIME: 3½ HOURS

YIELD: 8 HOT DOGS

DIETARY NOTES: DAIRY

CHILI CHEESE DOG

Crimson Viper and I haven't exactly seen eye to eye in the past, but her determination has always been so impressive to me. She told me once that her daughter Lauren keeps her motivated. I saw her share some pics on social media of them eating some delicious-looking chili cheese dogs. I was so jealous that I just had to make some for myself.

INGREDIENTS:

2 tablespoons canola oil

½ medium yellow onion, diced

2 shallots, diced

4 garlic cloves, diced

1 pound (454 g) ground turkey

2 teaspoons (6 g) salt

½ teaspoon (.5 g) black pepper

2 tablespoons (17 g) ground cumin

3 tablespoons (27 g) chili powder

1 tablespoon (18 g) brown sugar

1 teaspoon (5 ml) Worcestershire
    sauce

One 15-ounce (425 g) can diced
    tomatoes

3 tablespoons (55 g) tomato paste

1 bay leaf

8 hot dogs, cooked

8 hot dog buns, warmed

½ medium yellow onion, finely diced
    (for topping)

½ cup (117 g) shredded cheddar

Mustard

INSTRUCTIONS:

Place a deep pot over medium heat. Add the canola oil to the pan and cook onion and shallots for 5 minutes, until soft. Add garlic, and cook for 2 more minutes. Add the ground turkey, and cook until it has all browned. Add the salt, pepper, cumin, chili powder, brown sugar, and Worcestershire sauce. Mix until well combined. Add the tomatoes and tomato paste, and mix.

Add the bay leaf, cover, and reduce the heat to low. Simmer for 2 to 3 hours. The longer you let it cook, the more the flavors will infuse.

Place a cooked hot dog in a hot dog bun. Remove the bay leaf from the chili, and scoop a generous portion on top of the hot dog. Top with onion, cheddar, and mustard.

I've found that most types of ground meats work here!

DIFFICULTY:

PREP TIME: 1 HOUR

REST TIME: 3 TO 12 HOURS

COOK TIME: 30 MINUTES

YIELD: 4 TO 8 TORTAS

DIETARY NOTES: DAIRY

CARNE ASADA TORTAS

When the tournament passed through Mexico City, I had to make a stop at El Fuerte's taqueria. He wasn't competing, choosing instead to focus on his cooking, and I was quite surprised. The tortas were absolutely delicious, much better than some of his food I've had before—dare I say it tasted so great it sent me straight to heaven? His secret was that he decided to spend less time incorporating everyone's ideas and instead chose to perfect his own style.

FOR THE MEAT:

One 7-ounce (198 g) can chipotle peppers in adobo

1 jalapeño, stem removed and seeds removed (optional)

1 bunch fresh cilantro

4 garlic cloves

¼ medium red onion

¼ cup (59 ml) soy sauce

¼ cup (59 ml) canola oil, plus more for grill

Juice and zest of 1 orange

Juice and zest of 2 limes

2 tablespoons (30 g) brown sugar

1 tablespoon (8 g) ground cumin

2 tablespoons (17 g) chili powder

1 tablespoon (10 g) salt

½ teaspoon (.5 g) black pepper

2 pounds (907 g) skirt steak

FOR THE SANDWICHES:

Four 6-inch sandwich rolls

Refried beans

Shredded lettuce

Pickled Red Onion (page 29)

Tomato, sliced

Mayonnaise

½ avocado, sliced

TO MAKE THE MEAT:

Place the chipotle peppers with adobo, jalapeño, cilantro, garlic, and red onion in a blender. Blend until smooth. Add soy sauce, canola oil, orange juice and zest, lime juice and zest, brown sugar, cumin, chili powder, salt, and pepper. Mix until well combined. Transfer to a sealable bag. Add skirt steak, and toss until covered. Marinate in the refrigerator for at least 3 hours and up to 12 hours.

Preheat a grill. Oil the grate to prevent the steak from sticking. Cook directly over the heat until it has a nice char and has reached an internal temperature of 110°F (43°C), 5 to 10 minutes.

Transfer to a plate, and cover in aluminum foil. Allow the meat to rest for 10 minutes. Slice the meat against the grain to avoid pieces being chewy. Cover until you are ready to assemble the tortas.

TO ASSEMBLE:

Cut open a sandwich roll. On the bottom piece, spread the refried beans. Add the sliced skirt steak, followed by the shredded lettuce, Pickled Red Onion, and tomato.

On the top piece, spread a generous dollop of mayo. Lightly mash the avocado into the top part of the bun. Place the top piece of bread on the sandwich, and slice the sandwich in half, if desired. Assemble the other sandwiches and serve.

El Fuerte saw I was taking notes for my own recipe and suggested I replace the peppers with a few habaneros for that "extra spicy Habanero Dash!"

DIFFICULTY: ▬▬ ▬▬ ▬▬ ▬▬ ▬▬

PREP TIME: 30 MINUTES

YIELD: 6 DRINKS

DIETARY NOTES: GLUTEN-FREE, VEGAN

EL FUERTE DYNAMITE

El Fuerte and I talked about our mutual love for R. Mika over a refreshing agua fresca. I brought her up because of the R. Mika merchandise all over his restaurant, and he started naming all her special moves. I invited him to see one of her wrestling matches the next time he's in Japan. El Fuerte got so excited, he almost knocked over my drink.

INGREDIENTS:

½ cup (100 g) sugar
½ cup (118 ml) water
4 prickly pears
1 small watermelon
Juice of 2 limes, plus more if needed

INSTRUCTIONS:

Combine sugar and water in a small saucepan over medium-high heat. Whisk until the sugar has dissolved. Simmer for 5 minutes, and transfer to a large pitcher.

Remove the skin of the prickly pear. Cut the interior, transfer to a blender, and blend until smooth (seeds will still be whole). Pour through a fine mesh strainer into the pitcher to remove any seeds.

Cut out the interior of the watermelon, chop, and blend until smooth. Pour through a fine mesh strainer into the pitcher to remove any seeds.

Add the lime juice to the pitcher, and mix well. Taste and add additional lime juice if needed. Refrigerate for 2 hours to chill. The mixture can be stored for up to 1 week in the refrigerator. The juice will separate, so shake before serving.

If you can't find prickly pear, dragon fruit or kiwi work just as well.

DIFFICULTY:

PREP TIME: 1 HOUR

REST TIME: 12 TO 24 HOURS

COOK TIME: 1 HOUR

YIELD: 6 BAGELS

DIETARY NOTES: DAIRY-FREE, VEGETARIAN

EVERYTHING BAGEL

While catching up with Guile at the Air Force Base, he took me to his favorite local spot to get breakfast. I chuckled to myself because we went to the same place last time, too. Maybe it's the only place he goes? As we approached the counter, the merchant beamed and rang him up without waiting for an order. He turned to me and declared, "Guile always goes with the everything bagel." With a quick nod and the smallest hint of embarrassment, Guile paid and grabbed a seat for us. He clearly knows what he likes.

FOR THE DOUGH:

1 cup (237 ml) warm water (105°F to 110°F/40°C to 43°C)

1 tablespoon (22 g) honey

2½ cups plus 2 tablespoons (445 g) bread flour

1 tablespoon (12 g) vital wheat gluten

1½ teaspoon (5 g) diastatic malt powder (optional)

2 teaspoons (7 g) active dry yeast

2 teaspoons (8 g) salt

Neutral oil or nonstick spray, for oiling

FOR THE TOPPING:

1¼ tablespoons (10 g) dehydrated garlic flakes

1 tablespoon (8 g) dehydrated onion flakes

½ tablespoon (4.5 g) white sesame seeds

1 tablespoon (9 g) black sesame seeds

1 tablespoon (10 g) poppy seeds

½ tablespoon (7 g) flaky salt

FOR THE WATER BATH:

¼ cup (66 g) honey

8 cups (2 liters) water

FOR THE EGG WASH:

1 egg

1 tablespoon (15 ml) water

TO MAKE THE DOUGH:

Combine the water and honey. Whisk until the honey is dissolved. Combine 2½ cups of the bread flour, vital wheat gluten, diastatic malt powder, yeast, and salt in a bowl. Add the honey water to the dry ingredients, and mix until it just comes together. Once combined, let sit and rest for 5 minutes.

Transfer to a countertop, and knead. Add the remaining 2 tablespoons of bread flour while kneading. Knead for about 10 minutes. If the dough is still sticky, add additional flour. The end result will be a firm dough. Oil a bowl, place the dough in the bowl, and cover. Let rest in the refrigerator overnight, at least 12 hours.

Take the dough out of the refrigerator, split into 6 equal portions, and form into balls. Cover with a kitchen towel, and let rest for 20 minutes at room temperature.

TO MAKE THE TOPPING AND FORM THE BAGELS:

Combine all the ingredients for the topping in an airtight container. This can be stored for 2 months.

Line a baking sheet with parchment paper. Take a dough ball, and roll it out flat until it is about 1 inch thick. Take one end, and tightly roll the dough into a log. Using your hands, roll the log until it is 8 to 10 inches long. The ends should be slightly thinner than the center of the log. Take the log, and loop it around your hand. The ends should overlap with one another about 2 to 3 inches. Pinch it together. With your hand in the center of the bagel, carefully roll the 2 ends together on the counter until they just come together. Transfer to the baking sheet, and repeat with the remaining dough portions. Cover and let rest for another 30 minutes at room temperature.

Preheat oven to 425°F (220°C).

TO MAKE THE WATER BATH:

Combine the water and honey for the water bath in a large pot. Bring to a boil, then gently lower a few of the bagels into the hot water, but do not overcrowd the pot. Allow the bagels to boil for 30 seconds per side, and then remove and place back on the baking sheet. Boil all the bagels.

Continued on page 56 . . .

EVERYTHING BAGEL (CONTINUED)

TO MAKE THE EGG WASH AND ASSEMBLE:

Whisk together the egg and water, and brush each bagel with the egg wash.

Sprinkle a generous amount of the topping on each bagel. Bake for 18 to 20 minutes, rotating the pan halfway through to ensure that the bagels bake evenly.

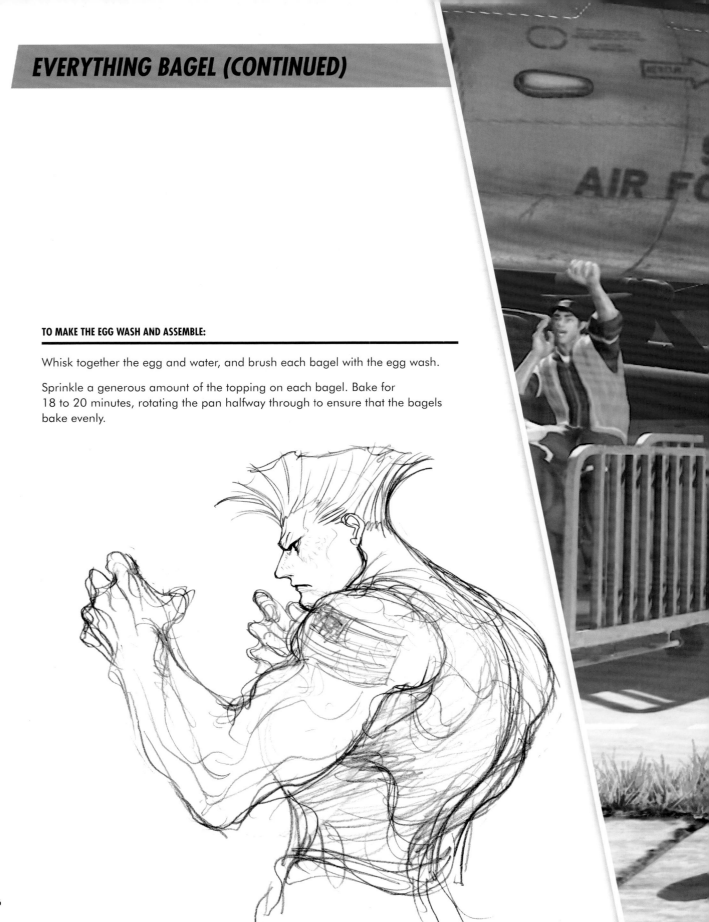

DIFFICULTY:

PREP TIME: 30 MINUTES

REST TIME: 8 TO 12 HOURS

YIELD: 2 DRINKS

DIETARY NOTES: GLUTEN-FREE, VEGAN

SONIC TEMPEST

I bought Guile a fancy coffee drink as a thanks for taking time to hang out. As I handed him the glass, he raised an eyebrow and grunted, "I take my coffee black." It took some convincing, but he eventually conceded and grudgingly gave it a try. "Hmm . . . not half bad. I guess I can try shaking things up from time to time."

INGREDIENTS:

4½ tablespoons (32 g) ground coffee

¼ teaspoon (.5 g) ground nutmeg

¼ teaspoon (.5 g) ground allspice

1 teaspoon (2 g) ground cinnamon

½ teaspoon (1 g) ground ginger

Pinch of salt

⅝ cup (150 g) hot water

1½ cups (350 g) cold water

INSTRUCTIONS:

Combine the ground coffee, nutmeg, allspice, cinnamon, ginger, and salt in an airtight container. Add the hot water, and lightly stir to combine. Let sit for 1 minute. Add the cold water. Cover, and let rest in the refrigerator for 8 to 12 hours.

Filter the coffee, and store in the refrigerator for up to 5 days. Serve with ice.

I can't believe I got Guile to try something new! What other coffee drinks might he like?

DIFFICULTY: ▬ ▬ ▬ ▬ ▭ ▭

PREP TIME: 45 MINUTES

COOK TIME: 45 MINUTES

YIELD: 4 SERVINGS

DIETARY NOTES: DAIRY

SPAGHETTI CARBONARA

I wanted to get a quick bite with Ken, but he insisted that I join him and his family for a home-cooked meal. When we arrived at his place, he introduced me to his adorable family, then rushed into the kitchen to prepare a batch of pasta. I had no idea Ken was also a master of the culinary arts!

INGREDIENTS:

1½ tablespoons (17 g) salt

1 whole egg plus 4 egg yolks

2 tablespoons (60 g) white miso

¾ cup (60 g) Parmesan cheese, plus more if needed

⅓ cup (30 g) Romano cheese, plus more if needed

2 teaspoons (4 g) black pepper, plus more if needed

1 pound (454 g) spaghetti

2 tablespoons (30 g) duck fat

8 ounces (228 g) duck bacon, cut into large pieces

4 garlic cloves, minced

1 nori sheet, sliced into thin strips

2 teaspoons (7 g) white sesame seeds

1 teaspoon (3.5 g) black sesame seeds

1 scallion, finely chopped

4 poached eggs, for topping

INSTRUCTIONS:

Heat water, enough to cover the pasta, in a large pot over high heat. When it comes to a boil, add the salt.

In a medium bowl combine the egg yolks, whole egg, miso, half of the Parmesan, half of the Romano cheese, and black pepper. Whisk together until well combined.

Cook the pasta until just al dente. Drain the pasta and reserve at least 2 cups of the water.

Heat a deep pot over medium heat. Add the duck fat and melt. Add the duck bacon and cook until crispy, about 6 to 10 minutes.

Add garlic and cook for another 2 minutes.

Add 1 cup of the pasta water and bring to a boil. Stir until the water begins to reduce. Add the pasta and stir together rigorously.

Remove the pot from the heat and continue to stir. Carefully pour the egg mixture in and keep stirring. It is important to keep stirring to not let the eggs scramble. Stir until the sauce appears glossy.

Stir in the remaining cheese. If the sauce is too thick, add additional pasta water to the pasta to help thin out the sauce. Make sure to add water in small portions so as not to make the sauce too runny. Taste and season with additional pepper or cheese if needed.

Mix the nori, white sesame seeds, black sesame seeds, and scallions in a bowl.

When serving a portion, place some pasta on a plate and top with a poached egg. Sprinkle with the nori mixture.

DIFFICULTY:

PREP TIME: 5 MINUTES

COOK TIME: 5 MINUTES

YIELD: 1 SERVING

DIETARY NOTES: DAIRY, VEGETARIAN

SHORYUKEN

Ken shared stories over dinner about how hard it was training under Gouken. He had to learn so many moves and techniques, just like Ryu! Ken even tried introducing Gouken to his favorite dessert, affogato, only for Gouken to improve on his technique with matcha instead of espresso. It just goes to show that there's always room to get stronger.

INGREDIENTS:

1½ teaspoons (3.7 g) matcha powder
⅓ cup (100 ml) water (175°F/79°C)
1 to 2 scoops vanilla ice cream
2 tablespoons (50 g) adzuki beans, cooked
2 matcha-flavored Pocky

INSTRUCTIONS:

Sift the matcha into a small bowl. Add the water, and whisk until there are no clumps.

Place the vanilla ice cream in a large cup. Top with adzuki, and pierce with the matcha Pocky. Pour the matcha over the ice cream.

(!) **Matcha ice cream would make for a wonderful double punch of green tea flavor.**

(!) **Many grocery stores now carry adzuki beans, but you can also get them online!**

DIFFICULTY: ▬▬ ▬ ▬ ▬ ▬ ▬
PREP TIME: 30 MINUTES
COOK TIME: 5 MINUTES
YIELD: 4 BURGERS
DIETARY NOTES: DAIRY

SMASH BURGERS

I had a great time with Poison watching a Metro City wrestling match that she was promoting. I honestly felt a little bad for the other contestants; no one stood a chance against Hugo. We celebrated his victory with some Smash Burgers on the way out, joking about how the burgers had it a lot easier than the poor wrestlers who got in Hugo's way. Don't skip making the sauce in this recipe—it's the real secret move!

FOR THE SAUCE:

½ cup (100 g) mayonnaise

2 tablespoons (30 g) ketchup

1 tablespoon (16 g) mustard

1 tablespoon (33 g) pickle relish, any kind

½ teaspoon (1 g) paprika

2 teaspoons (10 ml) pickle juice, any kind

½ teaspoon (1 g) black pepper

FOR THE BURGER:

4 burger buns

Butter, for buns

1 teaspoon (4 g) garlic powder

1 teaspoon (4 g) onion powder

2 teaspoons (11 g) salt

½ teaspoon (1 g) black pepper

1½ pounds (680 g) ground beef

Oil, for pan

8 slices American cheese

1 medium yellow onion, sliced and sautéed

1 medium tomato, sliced

Lettuce

TO MAKE THE SAUCE:

Combine all sauce ingredients in an airtight container, which can be stored in the refrigerator for up to 2 weeks.

TO MAKE THE BURGER:

Preheat the broiler. Prepare the burger buns by slicing and lightly buttering each side. Place under the broiler until golden brown. Generously slather some of the burger sauce on the bottom bun. Set aside until your burgers are cooked.

Combine garlic powder, onion powder, salt, and pepper in a small bowl. Split the ground beef into 3-ounce balls, about 8 total. Generously season each of the balls with the mixed spices.

Preheat a skillet over high heat for 2 minutes. Place a small amount of oil and a few balls of ground beef, making sure to not overcrowd the pan. Once placed, use a spatula to smash the burgers into thin patties. Cook until the bottoms start to brown, about 45 seconds.

Flip the burgers, and cover each patty with a slice of cheese. Cook until the cheese has melted. Stack the burgers 2 patties high. Transfer to the bottom bun slice. Top with sautéed onions, tomato, and lettuce.

DIFFICULTY: ━━ ━━ ━━ ━━ ━━

PREP TIME: 1 HOUR

COOK TIME: 30 MINUTES

YIELD: 3 SERVINGS

DIETARY NOTES: DAIRY-FREE, VEGETARIAN

FRIES

I made a big mistake ordering from the stall when I went out with Poison. She ordered ahead of me, and not remembering how much she loves French fries, I assumed one of her three orders of fries was for me. I was going to live with my miscalculation, but the fries smelled so good I had to swallow my pride and go back and order my own. This recipe approximates their savory and unique flavors.

INGREDIENTS:

3 russet potatoes, sliced into long
   strips
Peanut oil, for frying
1 teaspoon (4 g) garlic powder
½ teaspoon (1 g) onion powder
½ tablespoon (5.5 g) salt
1 teaspoon (1 g) black pepper
1 tablespoon (8 g) furikake

INSTRUCTIONS:

Place all the sliced potatoes in a bowl of cold water. Soak for at least 30 minutes, and keep in the water until you are ready to fry.

Pour 2 inches of peanut oil in a deep heavy-bottomed pot, and heat to 300°F (150°C). Remove the potatoes from the water, and dry well. Deep-fry the potatoes in batches for 5 minutes each. The potatoes will be soft but not browned.

Transfer to a wire rack and let the excess oil drain.

When all potatoes have been fried once, increase the oil's heat to 375°F (190°C). Combine the garlic powder, onion powder, salt, pepper, and furikake in a small bowl.

Fry the potatoes in batches again until they become golden brown, about 2 minutes each. Transfer back to a bowl, and generously season with the spice mix.

DIFFICULTY:
PREP TIME: 30 MINUTES
COOK TIME: 4½ HOURS
YIELD: 8 TACOS
DIETARY NOTES: DAIRY, PORK

CARNITAS

I didn't get a chance to catch up with T. Hawk after his match, but I noticed El Fuerte had "T. Hawk Tacos" at his taqueria. I had hoped to ask T. Hawk about what gives him strength, but El Fuerte had me covered. He went on and on about the struggles T. Hawk's people went through and the effort he made to give them better opportunities with his winnings.

INGREDIENTS:

4 pounds (1,814 g) skinless,
    boneless pork shoulder
1 medium yellow onion, quartered
1 tablespoon (11 g) salt
1 teaspoon (1 g) black pepper
1 tablespoon (10 g) chili powder
2 tablespoons (5 g) dried oregano
1 tablespoon (9 g) ground cumin
1 tablespoon (8 g) ground coriander
2 teaspoons (4 g) paprika
2 cinnamon sticks
2 bay leaves
10 garlic cloves, sliced
Juice of 2 limes
Juice of 1 orange
2 cups (473 ml) chicken stock

TO SERVE:

Corn tortillas
Avocado, sliced
Queso fresco
Pickled Red Onion (page 29)
Fresh cilantro, chopped
Radish, sliced
Lime, sliced into wedges
Tomatillo salsa

INSTRUCTIONS:

Preheat oven to 275°F (135°C). Cut the pork into large 2-inch chunks. Place the pork and onion in a Dutch oven. Add the spices and mix in well. Top with the garlic. Add the lime juice, orange juice, and enough chicken stock until the meat is just under three-quarters of the way covered. Keep uncovered, and place in the oven. Cook for 3 to 4 hours, mixing often.

Once the pork easily pulls apart, transfer the meat to an aluminum-foil-lined baking sheet. Gently pull apart the pork to shred the meat. Turn on the broiler, and place the sheet directly below it. Let the meat develop a crispy crust, flip, and allow to crisp up again.

Serve on corn tortillas with avocado, queso fresco, Pickled Red Onion, cilantro, radish, limes, and tomatillo salsa.

SOUTH AMERICA

DIFFICULTY:

PREP TIME: 10 MINUTES

COOK TIME: 5 TO 8 MINUTES PER BATCH

YIELD: 3 SERVINGS

DIETARY NOTES: VEGAN

PLATANOS MADUROS

Jimmy has always been a close friend and an excellent fighter, although you may know him by his alias, Blanka. He's passionate in the ring, but he's such a softy when he isn't fighting. He sometimes gets a little down when he starts missing his mother, but I've learned to take him out for some fried platanos to remind him of home. It's such a simple dish but oh so good.

INGREDIENTS:

2 plantains, very ripe
Salt
Vegetable oil, for frying

INSTRUCTIONS:

Prepare the plantains by cutting them open and slicing into ½-inch-thick pieces. Lightly salt the slices.

Pour ½ inch of oil into a frying pan, and heat over medium. Once heated, carefully add the plantains, and cook each side until golden, 2 to 3 minutes per side.

Drain on a paper-towel-covered plate, but don't leave them on the paper towel for long, or they can get stuck. Serve warm.

DIFFICULTY: ▬▬ ▬ ▬ ▬ ▬

PREP TIME: 25 MINUTES

COOK TIME: 45 TO 55 MINUTES

YIELD: 1 CAKE

DIETARY NOTES: DAIRY, VEGETARIAN

PINEAPPLE POUND CAKE

I haven't seen Jimmy since he visited me at work with his Blanka-chan plushies. Oh my gosh, those dolls are so cute! I just wish he didn't lose his cool and break one of the crane machines. If those Blanka-chans hadn't become so popular, I would have been in real trouble with my manager. Jimmy even brought over his favorite pineapple pound cake as an apology for making a mess of things.

FOR THE CAKE:

2½ cups (415 g) all-purpose flour

1 teaspoon (4 g) baking powder

½ teaspoon (1 g) salt

1 cup (227 g) unsalted butter, softened

1½ cups (300 g) sugar

3 eggs

1 teaspoon (5 ml) vanilla extract

1 cup (200 g) crushed pineapple, drained

⅓ cup (75 g) yogurt

⅓ cup (79 ml) coconut milk

Cooking spray, for pan

FOR THE GLAZE:

1½ cups (212 g) confectioners' sugar

2½ tablespoons (32.5 ml) lime juice

2 tablespoons (30 ml) pineapple juice

FOR THE TOPPING:

½ cup (100 g) fresh pineapple, chopped

Zest of 2 limes

TO MAKE THE CAKE:

Preheat oven to 350°F (180°C). Combine flour, baking powder, and salt in a medium bowl.

Combine the butter and sugar in a large bowl, and mix until smooth. Add the eggs and vanilla extract. Add half the flour mixture into the bowl, and mix well. Mix in the crushed pineapple, yogurt, and coconut milk. Add the remaining flour mixture, and mix until completely smooth.

Prepare a Bundt cake mold with cooking spray. Pour the batter into the mold, and bake for 45 to 55 minutes or until a toothpick comes out clean. Allow to cool completely.

TO MAKE THE GLAZE AND ASSEMBLE:

Combine the glaze ingredients in a small bowl. Pour over the cooled Bundt cake. Top with fresh pineapple and lime zest.

I like waiting to add the glaze until I'm actually serving this. Otherwise, it gets lost in the cake!

DIFFICULTY: ▬ ▬ ▬ ▬

PREP TIME: 1 HOUR

REST TIME: 12 HOURS

COOK TIME: 3 HOURS

YIELD: 4 TO 6 SERVINGS

DIETARY NOTES: DAIRY-FREE, PORK

FEIJOADA

Sean set up a lunch between Laura and me, but she wanted to fight first. She went up against Ryu in the past and wanted to see how his protégée held up. We ended in a draw, but I did not expect her to be so tough! Maybe all this eating has slowed me down? Afterward, Laura took me to share some feijoada, but she ate only the stew. I was left with all the collard greens and oranges.

FOR THE STEW:

1 pound (454 g) dried black beans
1 pound (545 g) pork spare ribs
3 bay leaves
2 ham hocks
4 bacon slices
1½ ounces (40 g) beef jerky
1 tablespoon canola oil
1 medium yellow onion, sliced
8 garlic cloves, minced
½ bundle fresh cilantro, chopped
3½ ounces (100 g) linguica, sliced
10 ounces (280 g) paio sausage, sliced
Salt
Black pepper

FOR THE COLLARD GREENS:

16 ounces (450 g) collard greens, stems removed and julienned
1 tablespoon (13.5 g) canola oil
4 garlic cloves, minced
1 cube chicken bouillon
Salt
Black pepper

FOR SERVING:

3 cups (1110 g) cooked rice
½ bundle fresh cilantro, chopped
1 orange, peeled and wedges split

TO MAKE THE STEW:

Place the dried black beans in a large bowl, and cover with water. Let sit overnight to soften the beans.

Drain, and transfer the beans to a large pot. Add the ribs, bay leaves, and enough water to just cover. Place over medium-high heat, and bring to a boil. Reduce the heat, and simmer for 1 hour. Make sure to skim any foam that forms at the top.

Add the ham hocks, bacon, and beef jerky. Simmer for another hour. Continue to remove any foam that forms at the top.

After the stew has finished simmering, place canola oil in a medium pan over medium-high heat for 1 minute. Add the onion and garlic. Cook until the onion has softened. Add the cilantro, and continue to cook until the onion has browned slightly. Add 2 ladlefuls of black beans and water. Thicken the stew by mashing the beans and onion using a masher, or place them in a blender and blend until smooth, and transfer to the large pot.

Remove the ham hocks, and add the linguica and paio sausage. Simmer for another 30 minutes or until the beans are completely softened and sausage is cooked. Add salt and pepper to taste.

TO MAKE THE COLLARD GREENS:

Place the greens in a large pot, cover with water, and simmer over medium-high heat for 30 minutes. Drain, and set aside.

Place canola oil in a large pan over medium-high heat. Add the garlic, and cook until softened, about 2 minutes. Crumble the chicken bouillon, and mix until completely dissolved. Add the boiled collard greens, and pan-fry until they are covered with garlic and chicken bouillon. Taste, and season with salt and pepper.

TO SERVE:

Prepare a plate by serving the feijoada over rice. Top with cilantro. Serve with a large helping of collard greens and orange slices on the side.

DIFFICULTY:

PREP TIME: 1½ HOURS

COOK TIME: 30 MINUTES

YIELD: 10 TO 15 COXINHAS

DIETARY NOTES: DAIRY

COXINHAS

Ken introduced me to his pupil, Sean, and suggested the two of us have a sparring match. Sean was convinced he could beat me when he heard I had trained with Dan for a time, so naturally I made sure to take him down a peg. But, to my surprise, he was pretty gracious in defeat and wanted to talk about my training over coxinhas.

FOR THE POACHED CHICKEN:

1 pound (454 g) chicken breast
Salt
4 cups (946 ml) chicken stock
1 carrot, roughly chopped
1 head garlic, halved
1 bay leaf

FOR THE FILLING:

1 tablespoon (15 ml) canola oil
1 medium yellow onion, sliced
2 garlic cloves, diced
2 teaspoons (8 g) salt
½ teaspoon (1 g) black pepper
2 teaspoons (5 g) paprika
2 tablespoons (28 g) tomato paste
6 ounces (170 g) cream cheese
3 tablespoons (7.5 g) fresh cilantro, chopped

FOR THE DOUGH:

3 cups (710 ml) chicken stock
1½ tablespoons (21 g) unsalted butter
3⅓ cups (503 g) all-purpose flour

FOR FRYING:

Peanut oil
2 eggs
1 tablespoon (15 ml) milk
2 cups (180 g) panko bread crumbs

TO MAKE THE POACHED CHICKEN:

Generously season the chicken breast with salt. Place the chicken breast, chicken stock, carrot, garlic, and bay leaf in a deep pot over medium heat, and simmer for 15 to 20 minutes or until the chicken is cooked through.

Set the chicken aside to cool. Reserve the stock, and toss the carrot, garlic, and bay leaf. Once the chicken is cool enough, shred it.

TO MAKE THE FILLING AND DOUGH:

Place a large pan over medium-high heat, and add oil and sliced onion. Cook until it just starts to soften, about 5 minutes. Add the garlic and shredded chicken.

Add the salt, pepper, paprika, tomato paste, cream cheese, and cilantro. Mix until well combined. Remove from the heat, and set aside.

To make the dough: Combine the chicken stock and butter in a large saucepan over medium-high heat. Bring to a boil. Gradually stir in the flour until the dough is well formed and no longer sticky. Remove from the heat, and transfer to a countertop. Carefully knead the dough by hand, or with a spatula if too hot, for about 5 minutes or until the dough is completely smooth. Place under a moist towel until you are ready to use.

TO ASSEMBLE:

Take a piece of dough between the size of a golf ball and a large egg. Roll into a ball. Flatten the dough, and place between a teaspoon and a tablespoon of filling in the center without overfilling it. Wrap into a pear shape, making sure there are no holes. Repeat with all dough and filling.

TO FRY:

Fill a deep pot with 3 inches of peanut oil, and heat over medium-high to 350°F (180°C).

Whisk together the eggs and milk in a medium bowl. Place the panko in another bowl. Place each of the coxinhas in the egg mixture, then cover in panko.

Once the oil has reached the desired temperature, carefully place several coxinhas in the oil, but do not overcrowd. Fry until golden brown, 5 to 8 minutes. Transfer to a plate covered with paper towels. Repeat in batches with the remaining coxinhas.

AFRICA AND THE MIDDLE EAST

DIFFICULTY: ▬ ▬ ▬

PREP TIME: 30 MINUTES

REST TIME: 2 TO 6 HOURS

COOK TIME: 10 MINUTES PER BATCH

YIELD: 4 TO 6

DIETARY NOTES: DAIRY-FREE, GLUTEN-FREE

KUKU CHOMA

I caught up with Elena at her university in Paris. She showed me the vibes of the city just like I showed her around Tokyo a few years ago. It was a lot of fun, but I forgot just how personable Elena is with complete strangers. She treats everyone she runs into like she's known them forever. She was even more friendly with the street vendor grilling up some kuku choma, one of her favorite foods from back home in Kenya. She was definitely a regular at that food stall!

INGREDIENTS:

1 red bell pepper

7 garlic cloves

2-inch (5-cm) piece fresh ginger, peeled

1 teaspoon (3 g) red chile flakes (optional)

Zest and juice of 2 limes, divided

3 tablespoons (30 ml) canola oil, divided, plus more for grill

1 tablespoon (8 g) ground cumin

1 teaspoon (2 g) ground coriander

2 teaspoons (4 g) paprika

2 teaspoons (6 g) salt

1 teaspoon (1 g) black pepper

5 pounds (2.25 kg) full chicken wings

INSTRUCTIONS:

Place the bell pepper, garlic, ginger, and red chile flakes in a food processor. Puree until smooth, and transfer to a large bowl. Add the zest and juice of 1 lime, 2 tablespoons canola oil, cumin, coriander, paprika, salt, and pepper, and mix together well.

Transfer about 2 tablespoons of the marinade into a separate airtight container, and mix with the remaining lime zest and juice, and remaining tablespoon of canola oil. Set aside in the refrigerator.

Place the chicken wings in the large bowl and toss to cover in the remaining marinade. Let rest covered in the refrigerator for at least 2 hours and up to 6 hours.

About 15 minutes before grilling, remove the chicken wings and reserved marinade from the refrigerator. Preheat a grill, and oil the grate to prevent the wings from sticking. Place the chicken wings directly over the heat. Baste the wings several times with the reserved marinade while they grill. Flip the wings occasionally until they have a nice char and have cooked through (chicken is done when it reaches an internal temperature of 165°F/74°C), 5 to 10 minutes. Transfer to a plate, and wrap in aluminum foil until it's time to serve.

DIFFICULTY:

PREP TIME: 30 MINUTES

COOK TIME: 10 MINUTES

YIELD: 8 EGGS

DIETARY NOTES: DAIRY-FREE, GLUTEN-FREE, VEGETARIAN

MAYAI PASUA

We swung by Elena's place after exploring the city, and I opened her fridge looking for something to drink. I don't know what I was expecting, but it wasn't a shelf full of hard-boiled eggs. Elena gets so lost in her studies sometimes that she needs a snack to fuel herself up, and these mayai pasua are a quick bite that does the trick!

FOR THE KACHUMBARI:

2 tomatoes, chopped
¼ medium red onion, diced
½ bunch fresh cilantro
Zest and juice of 2 limes
Salt
Black pepper

FOR THE EGGS:

8 eggs

TO MAKE THE KACHUMBARI:

Combine the tomatoes, red onion, cilantro, and lime zest and juice in a medium bowl. Season with salt and pepper to taste.

TO PREPARE THE EGGS:

Place the eggs in a large pot, and fill with enough water to completely cover them. Cover with a lid, and place over medium-high heat. Bring to a rapid boil for 8 minutes, then immediately take the pot off the stove, and place it under cold running water. Move the eggs to a bowl filled with ice cubes and water to quickly cool them. Once the eggs are cool, carefully peel them.

Carefully cut each hard-boiled egg vertically down the middle, but do not cut through the egg completely. Gently stuff the eggs with the kachumbari, and enjoy.

DIFFICULTY:

PREP TIME: 1 ½ HOURS

COOK TIME: 1 HOUR

YIELD: 6 TO 8 SERVINGS

DIETARY NOTES: VEGAN

KOSHARI

I spotted Menat in the crowd during one of the tournament stops and walked over to introduce myself. I was hoping to try my hand against someone with soul power, but Menat said she had some of her master's errands to run when the tournament was over, so we sat together and chatted as the matches went on. She was eating this delicious Egyptian dish called koshari and offered me some. Maybe she used her fortune-telling to know that I hadn't eaten all day? Either that or she heard my stomach rumble.

FOR THE CRISPY ONIONS:

2 medium yellow onions, sliced thin
3 tablespoons (30 g) all-purpose flour
1 tablespoon (12 g) salt
¼ cup (59 ml) canola oil

FOR THE TOMATO SAUCE:

1 tablespoon (15 ml) canola oil
1 cinnamon stick
1 bay leaf
½ medium yellow onion, chopped
5 garlic cloves, grated
2 cups (473 ml) tomato sauce
2 teaspoons (6 g) ground cumin
2 teaspoons (6 g) ground coriander
1 teaspoon (2 g) ground cayenne
  pepper
1 teaspoon (2 g) paprika
2 teaspoons (8 g) salt
1 teaspoon (1 g) black pepper

FOR THE RICE:

1 cup (180 g) basmati rice
1 tablespoon (14 g) unsalted butter
¼ medium yellow onion, diced
½ cup (45 g) vermicelli
2 cups (473 ml) vegetable broth
1 teaspoon (3 g) ground cumin
1 teaspoon (3 g) ground coriander
½ teaspoon (1.5 g) chili powder
½ teaspoon (1.5 g) paprika
1 teaspoon (4 g) salt

FOR SERVING:

1 cup (200 g) lentils, cooked
1 pound (454 g) elbow macaroni,
  cooked
One 15-ounce (439 g) can chickpeas

TO MAKE THE CRISPY ONIONS:

Toss the sliced onions in flour and salt. Place a large pan over medium heat. Add the canola oil and let it heat for about 1 minute. Cook the onions until crisp, 20 to 30 minutes.

TO MAKE THE TOMATO SAUCE:

Place the canola oil in a medium saucepan over medium-high heat. Add the cinnamon stick and bay leaf. Allow to toast for about 1 minute.

Add the onion and garlic, and cook until softened, about 5 minutes. Add the sauce and spices. Reduce the heat, and simmer for 15 minutes.

TO MAKE THE RICE:

Place the rice in a bowl, and cover with water. Let sit for 1 hour. Drain, and set aside.

Place the butter in a saucepan over medium heat until melted, then add the onion, and cook until translucent. Add the vermicelli, and toast for about 1 minute.

Add the rice, and cook until slightly toasted, about 3 minutes. Add the vegetable broth, cumin, coriander, chili powder, paprika, and salt. Bring to a boil, and then reduce the heat to low. Cover, and cook until the rice has cooked through, about 10 minutes.

TO SERVE:

Place a generous portion of rice on a plate. Top with lentils, macaroni, chickpeas, tomato sauce, and crispy onions.

DIFFICULTY: ▬ ▬ ▬ ▬ ▬ ▬ ▬

PREP TIME: 30 MINUTES

COOK TIME: 30 MINUTES

YIELD: 4 TO 6 SERVINGS

DIETARY NOTES: DAIRY, GLUTEN-FREE, VEGETARIAN

MOUTABEL

I asked Rashid for a quick bout, because we'd never fought before, but he politely declined and ran off like a stiff breeze. I chased him down, but phew, is he fast! It's a good thing I kept up with my cardio. He finally gave up and said he'd rather share meals with a friend than have a bout, so we had lunch at a market nearby. The roasted eggplant in the moutabel was something I'd never tasted before, and its smoky flavor was excellent.

INGREDIENTS:

2 medium eggplants
2 garlic cloves, crushed
¼ cup (70 g) tahini
3 tablespoons (46 g) Greek yogurt
2 tablespoons (30 ml) lemon juice
1½ tablespoons (22 ml) olive oil, plus
  2 tablespoons (30 ml) for garnish
½ teaspoon (1 g) paprika, plus more
  for garnish
1 teaspoon (5 g) salt, plus more if
  needed
¼ teaspoon (.5 g) black pepper, plus
  more if needed
1 tablespoon (3.5 g) fresh parsley,
  minced

INSTRUCTIONS:

If using a grill, preheat the grill on high to 400°F to 500°F (205°C to 260°C). Poke several holes in each eggplant, and rub with olive oil. Place the eggplants on the grill, and cook directly over the heat. Rotate occasionally, and cook until all sides are nicely charred and the insides are soft, 15 to 20 minutes. If using an oven, preheat to 425°F (220°C). Poke several holes in each of the eggplants, and rub with olive oil. Bake for 25 to 30 minutes, or until they have softened.

Place the cooked eggplants in a bowl, and cover. Let rest for 20 minutes, or until cool enough to peel. Peel and remove the skin and tops of the eggplants. If there are a lot of seeds on the inside, remove some of them. The seeds may give the dip a bitter flavor.

Transfer the eggplant into a food processor with the garlic and tahini. Pulse until the mixture is smooth. Transfer to a bowl.

Add the yogurt, lemon juice, olive oil, paprika, salt, and pepper. Mix together well. Taste and season with additional paprika, salt, and pepper to your liking.

Transfer to a serving plate. Garnish with parsley, olive oil, and paprika.

DIFFICULTY: ▬ ▬ ▬ ▬ ▬ ▬ ▬

PREP TIME: 1 HOUR

COOK TIME: 10 MINUTES

YIELD: 18 TO 22 PIECES

DIETARY NOTES: DAIRY-FREE

SHUMAI

I got an online message from Rashid asking if I wanted to join him at "the best shrimp shumai place in town." It may not be a dish native to his hometown, but he did tell me once that shrimp shumai was his favorite food. The shumai came out looking amazing, but he wouldn't let me touch any until he'd taken pictures for his social media fans. He took so long that the shumai got cold, so I made him buy me another order, and a piping hot steamer basket soon appeared.

INGREDIENTS:

2 garlic cloves

1-inch (2.5-cm) piece fresh ginger, peeled and sliced

½ lemongrass stalk, sliced

¾ pound (340 g) jumbo shrimp, peeled and deveined

2 scallions, white portion set aside and dark green portion sliced

¼ cup (50 g) water chestnuts

1 teaspoon (5 ml) soy sauce

2 teaspoons (10 ml) rice vinegar

½ teaspoon (2.5 ml) sesame oil

½ teaspoon (2 g) salt

¼ teaspoon (.5 g) black pepper

18 to 22 round dumpling wrappers

INSTRUCTIONS:

Place garlic, ginger, and lemongrass in a food processor. Pulse until finely ground. Scrape down the sides, add the shrimp, and pulse until just broken down. Add the white parts of the scallions along with the water chestnuts. Pulse until just combined. Add the soy sauce, rice vinegar, sesame oil, salt, and pepper. Pulse until it forms a smooth paste. Scrape down the sides occasionally to make sure everything is mixed in. Transfer to a medium bowl, and cover with a wet towel.

Place a dumpling wrapper on a counter, and scoop 1 to 2 tablespoons of filling in the center. Lightly wet your finger, and moisten the edges of the wrapper. Pinch the edges together until the wrapper surrounds the filling. Gently flatten the top of the filling to line up with the top edge of the wrapper. Place 2 slices of dark green scallion in the center. Set on a small piece of parchment paper, and place in a steamer basket, making sure to not overcrowd. Repeat with the remaining wrappers and filling.

Place water in a pot with a steamer basket and let it come to a boil. Place the basket of shumai over the boiling water, cover, and let steam for 8 to 10 minutes.

EUROPE

DIFFICULTY: ▬▬▬ ▭ ▭

PREP TIME: 1 HOUR

REST TIME: AT LEAST 2½ HOURS

COOK TIME: 1 HOUR

YIELD: 4 TO 8 PORTIONS

DIETARY NOTES: DAIRY, PORK

MAPLE BACON DOUGHNUTS

I've had some great bouts with Birdie in the past, but now I just see him lounging around Karin's place pretending like he's working. I wanted to know what sort of training he's been doing lately, but he just shrugged and offered me a doughnut from his pocket! I guess he isn't someone to look to for advice. I did eat the doughnut, and wow, was it good. Don't judge—this girl doesn't turn down sweet treats.

FOR THE CANDIED BACON:

Cooking spray
2 teaspoons (1 g) black pepper
¼ teaspoon (.5g) ground cayenne
  pepper
½ cup (85 g) light brown sugar
8 bacon slices

FOR THE DOUGHNUTS:

1 cup (237 ml) milk
6 tablespoons (90 g) unsalted butter
2¼ teaspoons (8 g) active dry yeast
2¼ cups (380 g) all-purpose flour
2¼ cups (380 g) bread flour
⅓ cup (67 g) sugar
1 teaspoon (3 g) salt
2 eggs
½ teaspoon (2.5 ml) vanilla extract
1 teaspoon (5 ml) maple extract
Neutral oil or nonstick spray,
  for oiling
Peanut oil, for frying

FOR THE ICING:

1 teaspoon (4 g) salt
1¾ cups (255 g) confectioners'
  sugar, plus more if needed
¼ cup (55 g) unsalted butter, melted
½ teaspoon (2.5 ml) maple extract
½ cup (155 g) maple syrup
1 tablespoon (15 ml) heavy cream
  (optional)

TO MAKE THE CANDIED BACON:

Preheat oven to 375°F (190°C). Wrap a baking sheet in aluminum foil, and place a layer of parchment paper on top. Coat with cooking spray.

In a small bowl, combine black pepper, cayenne, and brown sugar. Take each slice of bacon and thoroughly cover it in the spice mixture. Place the coated bacon on the baking sheet.

Bake for 10 minutes. Flip each piece over. Bake for 6 to 10 minutes more or until the bacon is crispy. Allow to cool. Chop into large pieces, and set aside.

TO MAKE THE DOUGHNUTS:

Combine the milk and butter in a medium saucepan over medium heat until the butter has melted. Take off the heat, and allow to cool to 100°F to 110°F (37°C to 43°C). Mix in the yeast, and let rest for 5 minutes, allowing the yeast to become active and frothy.

Combine the flours, sugar, and salt in a large bowl. Transfer half the flour mixture to the bowl of a stand mixer with a dough-hook attachment. Add the milk mixture, and mix until lightly incorporated. Add the eggs, vanilla extract, and maple extract, then the remaining flour mixture, and mix until combined. Knead until the dough is smooth, 5 to 10 minutes. Form into a ball, and transfer to a lightly oiled bowl. Cover, and allow the dough to rise for at least 2 hours or until it has doubled in size.

After the dough has risen, transfer to a lightly floured work surface. Punch the dough down and roll out to a ½-inch thickness. Cut doughnuts using 2 round cookie cutters—the large cutter should be about 3½ inches (8.75 cm). Cover with a damp kitchen towel, and let rest for at least 30 minutes, allowing the dough to rise again.

Bring a deep pot with 2 inches of peanut oil over medium heat to 350°F (180°C). Place the doughnuts in the oil, making sure not to overcrowd, and fry for 1 minute. Flip, then fry for another minute. Remove the doughnuts from the oil and place onto a plate covered with a paper towel. Repeat these steps with the remaining doughnuts and doughnut holes. The oil temperature might drop between each fry, so be sure to let the oil heat back up to 350°F (180°C) before each set. Allow the doughnuts to cool.

Continued on page 96 . . .

MAPLE BACON DOUGHNUTS (CONTINUED)

TO MAKE THE ICING AND ASSEMBLE:

Combine the salt and confectioners' sugar in a large bowl. Add the melted butter, maple extract, and maple syrup. Whisk together until smooth. If the icing is too thick, add the heavy cream. If the icing is too thin, add more confectioners' sugar.

Dip the top half of the cooled doughnuts into the icing. Top with the candied bacon, and allow the icing to set completely before serving.

The doughnut holes can be eaten plain, but I always ice them because the icing is so good!

DIFFICULTY: ▬ ▬ ▬ ▬ ▬ ▬

PREP TIME: 1½ HOURS

REST TIME: 3 TO 8 HOURS

COOK TIME: 45 MINUTES

YIELD: 4 TO 6 WRAPS

DIETARY NOTES: DAIRY

CHICKEN MASALA ROTI WRAP

Cammy took me to a pub she said she frequented with other groups of Delta Red, the special unit she's a part of. There were so many contrasting ingredients in the chicken masala roti wrap—from spicy to sweet and everything in between—that worked together to make a truly unique and delicious meal. I asked Cammy if she brought me to show me the strength of diversity working together toward a common goal, but she had no idea what I was talking about. It was just close to her workplace.

This is a big recipe with a lot of components, and sure, you can buy some of them, but there's nothing like making everything from scratch!

FOR THE CHICKEN MASALA:

2 pounds (907 g) boneless, skinless chicken thighs, cut into bite-size pieces

1 tablespoon (23 g) garlic paste

2 tablespoons (47 g) ginger paste

¼ cup (65 g) yogurt

Zest and juice of 1 lemon

1 tablespoon (9 g) garam masala

1 tablespoon (8 g) Kashmiri chile powder

2 teaspoons (4 g) ground turmeric

1 teaspoon (2 g) paprika

1 teaspoon (3 g) ground coriander

½ teaspoon (1 g) ground fenugreek

½ teaspoon (1 g) ground cumin

1 teaspoon (5 g) salt

½ teaspoon (1 g) black pepper

FOR THE ROTI:

1 cup (180 g) whole wheat flour

1 teaspoon (5 g) salt

1 teaspoon (5 ml) canola oil

½ cup (118 ml) warm water

FOR SERVING:

Mango Chutney (page 29)

Cucumber Raita (page 31)

Handful of fresh cilantro

Handful of butter lettuce

Pomegranate seeds

TO MAKE THE CHICKEN MASALA:

Combine all ingredients in a large bowl. Cover and marinate for 3 hours or up to 8 hours. While the masala is marinating, skip ahead to the roti instructions.

Soak the wooden skewers in water for 30 minutes prior to grilling. Remove the chicken from the marinade and place a few pieces on each skewer.

Preheat the grill on high heat. Grill the skewers until the chicken is cooked through (chicken is done when it reaches an internal temperature of 165°F/74°C), 5 to 10 minutes, flipping to crisp all sides. When serving in a roti, remove the skewers.

TO MAKE THE ROTI:

Combine flour and salt in a large bowl. Add the oil, and slowly add the water while mixing together. Knead for about 5 minutes, until soft and smooth. Cover with a damp towel, and let rest for 15 minutes.

Split into 4 to 6 equal pieces. Shape each into a ball, and cover again with a damp towel to keep the roti from drying out while you cook them.

Take one of the balls and roll out the dough until very thin. Set a cast-iron griddle over high heat. Do not add any oil. Place the rolled-out dough, and cook until bubbles start to form, about 1 minute. Flip and cook for another 15 seconds. Remove from the griddle and place directly over a flame. Flip and lightly brown both sides but be sure not to let the roti burn. Place in a sealed container to keep warm. Repeat the previous step and this one with the remaining dough.

TO ASSEMBLE:

Take a roti and add chicken masala to the center. Add a generous amount of Mango Chutney and Cucumber Raita. Top with cilantro, butter lettuce, and pomegranate seeds. Roll up the roti. You can fold a piece of foil around the bottom to keep the filling from falling out, but I eat them so quickly I don't need it!

DIFFICULTY: ▬ ▬ ▬ ▬ ▬

PREP TIME: 1 HOUR

COOK TIME: 30 MINUTES

YIELD: 24 TO 30 CUPCAKES

DIETARY NOTES: DAIRY, VEGETARIAN

KILLER BEE CUPCAKES

I spotted these sweet honey cupcakes on a walk with Cammy, and it reminded me that she used to go by the name Killer Bee. I asked her between mouthfuls how she found the strength to get away from her more sinister past self. She explained it wasn't her strength at all but the love and compassion of those around her. I was surprised to hear such a strong fighter proclaim her own weakness, but it was really inspiring.

FOR THE CUPCAKES:

3½ cups (540 g) cake flour
1 teaspoon (3 g) ground cardamom
2 teaspoons (8 g) baking powder
1 teaspoon (3 g) salt
1 cup (227 g) unsalted butter,
  room temperature
½ cup (100 g) sugar
1 cup (360 g) honey
2 eggs
2 teaspoons (10 ml) vanilla extract
1 cup (237 ml) almond milk
½ cup (120 g) sour cream
7 ounces (200 g) honeycomb,
  optional

FOR THE HONEY GLAZE:

½ cup (180 g) honey
3 tablespoons (40 g) brown sugar
¼ cup (56 g) unsalted butter
1 teaspoon (3 g) salt
½ teaspoon (2 g) cornstarch
1 teaspoon (5 ml) water

FOR THE FROSTING:

1 cup (225 g) cream cheese
½ cup (112 g) unsalted butter
3 tablespoons (45 ml) Honey Glaze
1 tablespoon (15 ml) vanilla extract
2 to 4 cups (240 to 480 g)
  confectioners' sugar
1⅓ teaspoons (15 g) yellow sprinkles
1 tablespoon (10 g) black sprinkles

TOOLS:

Stand mixer or electric hand mixer
Pastry bag and star tip

TO MAKE THE CUPCAKES:

Preheat oven to 350°F (180°C). Combine the cake flour, cardamom, baking powder, and salt in a medium bowl, and set aside. In a large bowl using a stand mixer or an electric hand mixer set on medium speed, cream the butter and sugar. Add honey and then the eggs 1 at a time. Add vanilla extract, and mix well.

Add half the flour mixture to the large bowl, and blend until smooth. Add the almond milk, and blend. Add the remaining flour, and mix together. Finally, add the sour cream, and mix until it just comes together.

Divide the batter among cupcake tins (about two-thirds full). Bake for 15 to 17 minutes. Remove from the tins, and allow them to cool fully.

Optional: With a sharp knife, take each cupcake and cut a small cone out of the top center. Cut the bottom of the cone to make room for the honeycomb. Add a small piece of honeycomb and then top with the removed cupcake. The frosting will cover up the cut you made.

TO MAKE THE HONEY GLAZE:

Combine the honey, brown sugar, butter, and salt in a saucepan over medium heat until the butter has just melted. Combine the cornstarch and water in a small bowl. Add to the pan, and whisk in. Set aside, and allow to cool.

TO MAKE THE FROSTING AND ASSEMBLE:

Place the cream cheese and butter in a large bowl using a stand mixer or an electric hand mixer set on medium-high speed. Add the honey glaze and vanilla extract. Once the cream cheese and butter are well mixed, begin to slowly add the confectioners' sugar.

Add the confectioners' sugar until the frosting has thickened and is as sweet as you would like it. Transfer to a pastry bag with a star tip. Combine the yellow and black sprinkles in a small bowl.

Frost the cooled cupcakes. Top with a drizzle of honey glaze and sprinkles.

DIFFICULTY: ━━ ━━
PREP TIME: 15 MINUTES
COOK TIME: 30 MINUTES
YIELD: 2 CUPS
DIETARY NOTES: DAIRY, GLUTEN-FREE,
VEGETARIAN

ROLLING THUNDER

Whenever I spend time with Dudley, I can always expect two things: a bouquet of roses and an invitation for tea. I honestly have no idea how he juggles such tiny teacups with his vibrant boxing gloves, but he makes it look both graceful and effortless. When he's looking to change up his afternoon tea, he whips up a batch of this tea latte.

FOR THE JUNIPER AND CARDAMOM SYRUP:

½ cup (118 ml) water
½ cup (100 g) sugar
¼ cup (66 g) honey
1½ tablespoons (9 g) juniper berries
3 green cardamom pods

FOR THE TEA:

1 Earl Grey tea bag
2 cups (473 ml) water
1 cup (236 ml) milk
1 lemongrass stalk
1½ to 3 tablespoons (22 to 45 ml) Juniper and Cardamom Syrup
1 teaspoon (5 ml) vanilla extract
Pinch of salt
Pinch of ground cardamom

TO MAKE THE SYRUP:

Combine all the ingredients in a saucepan and place over medium-high heat. Whisk until the sugar has dissolved, and bring to a boil. Reduce the heat to medium-low, and simmer for 10 minutes. Remove from the heat, and let sit for 10 minutes. Strain into an airtight container. Once cooled, cover and store in the refrigerator for up to 2 weeks.

TO MAKE THE TEA:

Place the tea bags in a large cup. Pour in the boiling water. Brew the tea for 8 to 10 minutes. In a saucepan over medium heat, add the milk, lemongrass, and syrup, and bring to a simmer for 10 minutes. Remove from the heat, and whisk in the vanilla extract, salt, and cardamom. Pour the brewed tea into 2 cups, and fill each glass with the flavored milk.

DIFFICULTY: ▬ ▬ ▬ ▬ ▬

PREP TIME: 1 HOUR

REST TIME: 20 MINUTES TO 2 HOURS

COOK TIME: 45 MINUTES TO 1 HOUR

YIELD: 28 TO 32 DUMPLINGS

DIETARY NOTES: DAIRY, PORK

PIEROGIES

I watched Kolin's match and was mesmerized by her waves of ice. I wanted to know how she does it, so I asked around and found out pierogies are one of her favorite foods. I picked up an order and found her reading a book. I offered them and asked to chat, but she looked up from her book, down at the pierogies, back up at me, then froze them on the spot. What a jerk. Well ... joke's on her, now I can just enjoy them later!

FOR THE DOUGH:

3 cups (405 g) all-purpose flour
1 teaspoon (4 g) salt
2 large eggs
¼ cup (65 g) sour cream
½ to ¾ cup (118 ml to 177 ml) water

FOR THE FILLING:

2 large russet potatoes, peeled and cubed
3 tablespoons (42 g) unsalted butter
2 tablespoons (30 ml) milk, plus more if needed
¼ cup (58 g) cream cheese
1 cup (120 g) shredded cheddar
Salt
Black pepper

FOR THE TOPPING:

2 bacon slices, chopped
4 cremini mushrooms, sliced
200 g sauerkraut

FOR FRYING AND SERVING:

2 tablespoons (28 g) unsalted butter
Sour cream

TO MAKE THE DOUGH:

Combine flour and salt in a medium bowl. Mix in the eggs 1 at a time. Mix in the sour cream and ½ cup of water. Add more water only if the dough has not fully come together. Transfer the dough to a floured work surface, and knead for about 5 minutes. Wrap in plastic, and let rest at room temperature for at least 20 minutes but no longer than 2 hours.

TO MAKE THE FILLING:

Place the potato cubes in a pot, and cover with water.

Bring to a boil, and cook until the potatoes are soft. Drain the potatoes, and transfer to a bowl with butter. Mash until smooth. Add the milk and cream cheese. Mix until smooth. Fold in the cheddar, and season with salt and pepper to taste. As you are mashing, add more milk to give the potatoes an even smoother texture.

TO MAKE THE TOPPING:

Sauté bacon in a medium pan over medium-high heat for about 2 minutes. Add the mushrooms, and cook until the bacon and mushrooms have crisped up, 5 to 8 minutes. Add the sauerkraut, and cook until it has warmed and blended with the mushroom and bacon. Place in a bowl, and set aside.

TO ASSEMBLE:

Roll out the dough to ¼-inch thickness. Cut the dough using a 3- to 4-inch cutter. Place 1 tablespoon of the filling at the center of a cut dough piece. Wet your finger with water, then wet the edges of the dough. Fold over one edge, and press the edges together. Repeat until you have used all the dough and most of the filling.

Place the assembled pierogies into a pot of boiling water. Allow them to cook until they rise, 1 to 2 minutes. Remove from the water.

TO FRY AND SERVE:

When all have been cooked, place a medium or large pan with butter over medium-high heat. After the butter has melted, place the boiled pierogies in the pan. Cook until they brown, flip, and cook until the other side has browned. Serve with topping and sour cream.

DIFFICULTY: ▬▬ ▭ ▭ ▭ ▭

PREP TIME: 10 MINUTES

YIELD: 2 DRINKS

DIETARY NOTES: GLUTEN-FREE, VEGAN

AURA SOUL SPARK

I was walking down the streets of Venice when I had a chance encounter with Rose. I had seen her fight before, but this time she was lounging behind a table with a deck of tarot cards and a glass of sherry. "You're looking for your own strength, right? I can point you in the right direction if you'd like." But I turned Rose down. I told her I was trying to find my own answer, and if someone else told me, it would feel like a hollow victory. She just glanced at her cards, chuckled to herself, and wished me luck.

INGREDIENTS:

Ice

1 ounce (30 ml) sherry

1 ounce (30 ml) Italian bitter apéritif

½ ounce (15 ml) simple syrup

8 ounces (237 ml) blood orange
   Italian soda

2 orange peel slices

INSTRUCTIONS:

Fill a cocktail shaker with ice. Add the sherry, apéritif, and simple syrup. Cover, and shake for 10 seconds.

Divide the mixture from the shaker minus the ice into 2 chilled glasses with fresh ice. Top each with 4 ounces of blood orange Italian soda and an orange peel.

DIFFICULTY:

PREP TIME: 1 HOUR

REST TIME: 1 TO 4 HOURS

COOK TIME: 15 MINUTES

YIELD: 8 TO 10 SKEWERS

DIETARY NOTES: DAIRY

SOUVLAKI

I made a stop in Greece to see the fights there, but I didn't expect to run into Rashid. Like always, he was just dying to try another trendy food place, this time to order some souvlaki, so I joined him for lunch. A local paper had some new story about another mess Urien was causing in the area, but Rashid warned me not to get involved. Obviously I don't want anything to do with that person, but Rashid uncharacteristically got serious and made me promise.

INGREDIENTS:

⅓ cup (79 ml) olive oil

3 tablespoons (45 ml) red wine vinegar

Zest and juice of 2 lemons

1 head garlic (30 g), finely minced

1 tablespoon (3 g) dried oregano

2 tablespoons (10 g) fresh parsley

1 teaspoon (4 g) sugar

2 teaspoons (8 g) salt

½ teaspoon (1.5 g) black pepper

3 boneless, skinless chicken breasts, cut into cubes

8 to 10 wooden skewers

½ medium red onion, cut into bite-size pieces

1 bell pepper, cut into bite-size pieces

Tzatziki (page 31), for serving

Pita bread, for serving

INSTRUCTIONS:

Combine the olive oil, vinegar, lemon zest and juice, garlic, oregano, parsley, sugar, salt, and pepper in a large bowl. Whisk together until the sugar has dissolved. Transfer to a sealable plastic bag, and toss in the chicken. Refrigerate for at least 1 hour and up to 4 hours.

Soak the wooden skewers in water for 30 minutes prior to grilling. Remove the chicken from the marinade. Place 1 piece of chicken on a skewer followed by 2 pieces of red onion and a piece of bell pepper. Repeat until you have 4 pieces of chicken on the stick. Repeat to complete skewers.

Preheat the grill, and cook skewers for 5 to 10 minutes, flipping to crisp all sides. Serve with Tzatziki and pita bread.

DIFFICULTY:
PREP TIME: 30 MINUTES
YIELD: 4 SERVINGS
DIETARY NOTES: DAIRY, VEGETARIAN

HORIATIKI

The store owner overheard me and Rashid talking about Urien and came over, warning us in a hushed tone to keep quiet. He told us not to mention Urien or his brother Gill, who is just as much of a tyrant, and offered us a plate of horiatiki for listening to his concerns. I don't know what I stumbled into, but I definitely wasn't planning on approaching either of them. I'm trying to find what makes others strong, not the destruction that those two throw around.

INGREDIENTS:

1 teaspoon (3 g) salt

½ teaspoon (.5 g) black pepper

2 teaspoons (3 g) finely chopped fresh mint

1 tablespoon (3 g) dried oregano

2 garlic cloves, finely minced

¼ cup (59 ml) olive oil

2 tablespoons (30 ml) red wine vinegar

1 tablespoon (15 ml) lemon juice

1 cucumber, peeled and cut into half-slices

10 cherry tomatoes, halved

½ bell pepper, seeds removed and thickly sliced

¼ medium red onion, sliced

20 kalamata olives, pitted and halved

7 ounces (200 g) block feta cheese

INSTRUCTIONS:

Combine the salt, pepper, mint, oregano, garlic, olive oil, vinegar, and lemon juice in a large bowl. Whisk together well.

Add the cucumber, tomatoes, bell pepper, red onion, and olives. Toss until well coated with the dressing. Top with the block of feta cheese, and dig in!

DIFFICULTY:

PREP TIME: 15 MINUTES

YIELD: 2 SANDWICHES

DIETARY NOTES: DAIRY, PORK

BOCADILLO

I didn't expect to come across Cammy on my visit to Spain, but I'll never turn down a chance to catch up with her. She was competing in the local tournament, because she wanted to collect information on Vega's whereabouts, but the best she could find was the spot with the best bocadillo in town. I know it isn't what she was hoping for, but I made very good use of the intel she worked hard to get!

INGREDIENTS:

1 baguette

1 tomato, halved

3 tablespoons (45 ml) extra virgin
   olive oil

Salt

10 ounces (285 g) jamón serrano
   or prosciutto

6 ounces (170 g) Manchego cheese

INSTRUCTIONS:

Slice open the baguette lengthwise. Rub the interior of each side with the tomato. Brush the olive oil on each side, and sprinkle with salt. Top the bottom portion with jamón serrano and Manchego. Place the top slice of bread on the sandwich, cut into 2 portions, and serve.

DIFFICULTY: ▬▬▬▬ ▬▬ ▬▬▬

PREP TIME: 45 MINUTES

COOK TIME: 30 MINUTES

YIELD: 18 TO 24 CHURROS

DIETARY NOTES: DAIRY, VEGETARIAN

CHURROS

Cammy was disappointed she didn't find out more about Vega's location, so I bought some churros to cheer her up. She thought I was just hungry, but I surprised her by putting churros between my fingers to form a churro claw. I did my best Vega impression, talking about how beautiful I was and how much I was in love with myself. I thought I was spot on, but Cammy pointed out I needed a mask to get it right.

FOR THE CHURROS:

2 cups (300 g) all-purpose flour
1½ teaspoon (3 g) ground cinnamon
1½ cups (355 ml) milk
6 tablespoons (84 g) unsalted butter
1 teaspoon (4 g) salt
1 tablespoon (13 g) sugar
1 vanilla bean, halved
Peanut oil
2 eggs

FOR THE SPICE TOPPING:

½ cup (100 g) sugar
2 teaspoons (5 g) ground cinnamon
½ teaspoon (1 g) ground cardamom
¼ teaspoon (.5 g) salt

FOR THE DIPPING SAUCE:

1 cup (180 g) dark chocolate, chopped
¾ cup (177 ml) heavy cream
¼ cup (90 g) dulce de leche
1 tablespoon (14 g) unsalted butter
1 teaspoon (3 g) salt

TOOLS:

Pastry bag with large star tip
Deep-fry thermometer

TO MAKE THE CHURROS:

Combine the flour and cinnamon in a small bowl.

Combine the milk, butter, salt, sugar, and vanilla bean in a medium saucepan over medium-high heat. Bring to a boil. Reduce the heat, and simmer for 10 minutes. Turn off the heat, and remove the vanilla bean. Scrape the vanilla bean, and place the seeds in the heated milk. Add the flour mixture, and mix with a spatula until it forms a smooth dough and there are no clumps of raw flour. Allow the dough to cool.

While the dough is cooling, pour 1½ inches of peanut oil in a deep pot. Heat to 350°F (180°C) .

TO MAKE THE SPICE TOPPING AND FRY THE CHURROS:

On a plate, combine the sugar, cinnamon, cardamom, and salt. Set aside.

Once the dough has cooled, mix in the eggs 1 at a time until completely smooth. Transfer the dough to a pastry bag with a large star tip.

Preheat oven to 200°F (93.3°C). After the oil has heated, squeeze a 4- to 7-inch (10- to 18-cm) strip of dough into the hot oil. If the dough is sticking to the end, use a knife to cut it from the star tip. Use a pair of tongs to shape the churro into a straight line. Fry the churros for about 1½ minutes, flip, and fry for another minute or until they are golden brown.

Transfer the fried churro onto a plate lined with paper towels to remove any excess oil. Once the churro is cool enough to handle, toss it in the spice topping. Repeat the previous two steps until all the dough is fried. Keep the churros warm in the oven for up to 1 hour. These are best enjoyed the day they are made.

TO MAKE THE DIPPING SAUCE:

Combine the dark chocolate, heavy cream, dulce de leche, butter, and salt in a medium saucepan over medium-high heat until everything is well combined.

DIFFICULTY: ━━

PREP TIME: 1 HOUR

COOK TIME: 45 MINUTES

YIELD: 4 TO 6 BOWLS

DIETARY NOTES: DAIRY, GLUTEN-FREE, VEGETARIAN

BORSCHT

When I traveled to Russia, I caught one of Zangief's matches. R. Mika is my favorite wrestler, but Zangief can certainly put on a show. I found him after his bout, and we bought matching bowls of borscht, his favorite Russian delicacy. But when we went back to our seats to watch the next match, Zangief's excitement got the better of him and his cheering spilled my borscht all over my clothes. I'm pretty sure that outfit is lost—those stains are never coming out.

INGREDIENTS:

2 tablespoons (28 g) unsalted butter ⓘ
1 medium yellow onion, chopped
2 medium carrots, peeled and diced
2 celery stalks, minced
3 garlic cloves, minced
3 large beets, peeled and grated
4 tablespoons (75 g) tomato paste
1 teaspoon (4 g) sugar
5 medium Yukon Gold potatoes
7 cups (1656 ml) vegetable broth
1 bay leaf
½ medium cabbage, thinly sliced
1 tablespoon (15 ml) white vinegar
1 tablespoon (15 ml) lemon juice
Salt
Black pepper
Sour cream, for serving
Fresh parsley, for serving

INSTRUCTIONS:

Melt the butter in a large pot over medium-high heat. Add the onion, carrot, and celery, and cook until softened, about 5 minutes. Add the garlic. Stir and cook for 5 minutes.

Add the beets, tomato paste, and sugar. Cook for another 10 minutes, until beets are softened. Add potatoes, vegetable broth, and bay leaf, and bring to a boil. Reduce the heat, cover, and simmer for 20 minutes.

Add the cabbage, and simmer for another 15 minutes, or until the cabbage and potatoes are softened. Add the white vinegar and lemon juice. Season with salt and pepper to taste.

Divide among bowls for serving, and top each with sour cream and parsley.

ポイント！
ⓘ **Swapping the butter for coconut oil and the sour cream for a dairy-free option makes this recipe vegan!**

ASIA

DIFFICULTY: ▰▰▱▱▱

PREP TIME: 30 MINUTES

COOK TIME: 40 MINUTES

REST TIME: 12 HOURS OR OVERNIGHT

YIELD: 2 SERVINGS

DIETARY NOTES: GLUTEN-FREE, VEGAN

KHAO NIAOW MA MUANG

I really enjoy catching up with Adon, because he always treats me to a delicious bowl of mango sticky rice, but every conversation goes back to Sagat. Sagat this, Sagat that. Hey, Adon, how do you stay focused on aiming for the top? Two sentences later, and he's rambling about Sagat again! He's never going to beat Ryu if he's stuck in the past like that. At least he was too distracted to notice I swapped bowls with him when I finished mine so I could have more of this delicious sweet dish!

INGREDIENTS:

2 cups (450 g) Thai sweet rice

One 15-ounce (444 ml) can coconut
   milk

2 teaspoons (7.5 g) salt, divided

½ cup (100 g) sugar

¼ cup (58 g) brown sugar

1 teaspoon (3.8 g) cornstarch

1 tablespoon (15 ml) water

2 teaspoons (6.5 g) black sesame
   seeds

2 large mangoes, peeled and sliced

INSTRUCTIONS:

Place the sweet rice in a medium bowl, and cover with water. Rub the rice between your hands. The water will become quite cloudy. Drain, and repeat 3 more times. Fill the bowl again with water, and let soak overnight at room temperature.

Drain the rice, transfer to a cheesecloth, and wrap the rice.

Pour about an inch or two of water into a pot large enough to fit a steamer basket. Bring to a boil. Place the steamer basket on top, and place the cheesecloth on one side, leaving space for steam to rise. Cover the pot, and steam for 25 to 30 minutes.

While the rice is steaming, combine coconut milk, 1 teaspoon salt, and sugars in a medium saucepan over medium heat until sugar has dissolved. Keep warm.

Once the rice is done steaming, transfer to a heatproof bowl, and pour half the coconut mixture over the rice. Mix together, cover, and let sit for 25 minutes.

Combine the cornstarch and water in a small bowl. Reheat the sweet coconut milk, and whisk in the cornstarch slurry until it thickens to create a coconut syrup.

To serve, mix the rice again to fluff, and spoon a portion onto a plate or bowl. Top with coconut syrup, black sesame seeds, and mango slices.

DIFFICULTY:
PREP TIME: 1 HOUR
REST TIME: 1 TO 8 HOURS
YIELD: 5 SANDWICHES
DIETARY NOTES: DAIRY, VEGETARIAN

FRUIT SANDO

On one of my stops in Japan, my stomach started growling at me, so I followed my nose to the first street vendor I could find. The stall displayed a variety of mouthwatering fruit sandos, all fluffy and colorful. I handed over my payment, and as I looked up at the vendor, I was shocked to see blazing red eyes under a mane of red hair. It was Akuma selling fruit and other things, but he just nodded and took my coins. This is his recipe for what he says is his best-selling fruit sando.

FOR THE WHIPPED CREAM:

2½ cups (591 ml) heavy cream
2 tablespoons (26 g) sugar
2 teaspoons (10 ml) vanilla extract

FOR THE SANDWICH:

1 loaf Japanese Milk Bread
   (page 23)
6 strawberries, hulled and halved
2 kiwi, peeled and quartered
2 tangerines, peeled and slices
   separated
8 grapes, halved

TO MAKE THE WHIPPED CREAM:

Combine the heavy cream, sugar, and vanilla extract in a large cold bowl. Whisk together until stiff peaks form. Set aside.

TO ASSEMBLE THE SANDWICH:

Remove the heels of the loaf, leaving only the fluffy center. Cut the remaining loaf into 10 equal slices.

Spread an even layer of whipped cream on 5 slices of bread. Arrange the fruit on top of the whipped cream, making sure the center fruit will be cut cleanly in half when the sandwich is sliced. Cover the fruit with the remaining whipped cream.

Top each sandwich with the remaining slices of bread, making note of how the fruit is laid out. Tightly wrap each sandwich in plastic wrap, and make a mark on the wrap to indicate how to cut the sandwich so you can cleanly bisect the fruit in the middle. Refrigerate for at least 1 hour or up to 8 hours. Carefully cut the sandwiches in half diagonally. Remove the plastic wrap, and gently cut off the crust.

DIFFICULTY: ▭▭▭▭▭

PREP TIME: 30 MINUTES

REST TIME: 2 HOURS

COOK TIME: 20 MINUTES

YIELD: 6 DRINKS

DIETARY NOTES: DAIRY-FREE, VEGETARIAN

GOHADOKEN

After my duel with Ryu, we stopped by a local place for drinks. He ordered a sangria, fruit immersed in a beautiful red swirl. He stared at it for a bit, then gave me a few words of warning about the fighting style I've been honing. Using Akuma as a cautionary tale, he warned of the murderous intent, the Satsui No Hado, that he's always struggled with. The negative effects can grow stronger, similar to how the fruit in sangria that grows more alcoholic the longer it sits. I was really touched by Ryu's concern for me.

INGREDIENTS:

2 green cardamom pods
1 cinnamon stick
¼ cup (83 g) honey
¼ cup (50 g) sugar
½ cup (118 ml) water
1 lemongrass stalk, crushed and
  halved
3 medium peaches, sliced
2 small plums, sliced
1 large grapefruit, sliced
One 750-ml bottle sake

INSTRUCTIONS:

Combine the cardamom, cinnamon stick, honey, sugar, and water in a saucepan, and place over medium-high heat. Whisk until the sugar has dissolved, and bring to a boil.

Reduce the heat, and simmer for 10 minutes. Remove from the heat, and strain into a pitcher. Allow to cool completely.

Add the lemongrass and fruit to the pitcher. Mix until the fruit is covered in simple syrup.

Add the sake, and refrigerate for 2 hours before serving. Store in the refrigerator for up to 5 days.

DIFFICULTY: ▬▬ ▬ ▬ ▬ ▬

PREP TIME: 45 MINUTES

COOK TIME: 15 MINUTES

YIELD: 4 SERVINGS

DIETARY NOTES: DAIRY-FREE, PORK

MAPO TOFU

I asked Chun-Li how Li-Fen was doing. I hadn't seen her in a while, but it sounds like Li-Fen is as strong and independent as ever. Chun-Li was reluctant to share a few pictures of some amazing-looking mapo tofu they prepared together. I've never known Chun-Li to be much of a cook, but she told me Li-Fen brought the dish back from catastrophe. Chun-Li may be teaching Li-Fen martial arts, but I think she could learn something from Li-Fen about cooking!

INGREDIENTS:

2 teaspoons (5 g) Sichuan
   peppercorns
1 star anise
½ teaspoon (1 g) fennel seeds
2 whole cloves
5 dried red chiles
2 teaspoons (8 g) sugar
¼ cup (75 g) doubanjiang
1 teaspoon (5 ml) sesame oil
2 teaspoons (10 ml) Shaoxing wine
1 teaspoon (5 ml) soy sauce
   cup (160 ml) chicken broth
2 tablespoons (30 ml) oil
2 scallions, minced, dark green part
   separated from other parts
4 garlic cloves, minced
1-inch (2.5-cm) piece fresh ginger,
   peeled and minced
1 pound (454 g) ground pork
2 tablespoons (30 ml) water
2 teaspoons (5 g) cornstarch
14 ounces (397 g) firm tofu, cut into
   bite-size cubes

INSTRUCTIONS:

Place the peppercorns, star anise, fennel seeds, cloves, and chiles in a spice grinder or mortar and pestle, and blend until the peppercorns are well ground. Transfer to a bowl, combine with the sugar, and set aside.

In a small bowl, combine the doubanjiang, sesame oil, Shaoxing wine, soy sauce, and chicken broth. Set aside.

Place canola oil in a large stainless steel pan or wok over high heat. Add the light part of the scallions, garlic, and ginger. Cook until the garlic softens. Add ground pork and the spice blend, and mix together. Cook until the pork is cooked through. Add the sauce mixture, and combine. Let simmer for 3 minutes.

Whisk together the water and cornstarch in a small bowl. Add to the pan, and mix until the sauce has thickened.

Gently stir in the tofu. Cook for 3 to 5 minutes or until the tofu has heated through. Serve on top of a bowl of rice.

DIFFICULTY: ▬ ▬ ▬ ▬ ▬▬

PREP TIME: 30 MINUTES

REST TIME: 2 HOURS

COOK TIME: 45 MINUTES

YIELD: 8 TO 10 CREPES

DIETARY NOTES: DAIRY, VEGETARIAN

CREPES

I asked Chun-Li how she prepares herself for her matches and investigations. She told me she'd let me in on her secret and motioned for me to follow. She took me to this adorable crepe shop where everyone knew her name. We sat down and enjoyed crepes filled with a unique blend of grapefruit and cream cheese, but I had to nudge Chun-Li to share the details. How did she become the strongest woman in the world? She motioned to the desserts in front of us, winked, and said, "Strong motivation goes a long way."

FOR THE BATTER:

1 cup (160 g) all-purpose flour
½ teaspoon (1 g) ground cardamom
Pinch of salt
1 cup (237 ml) milk
¼ cup (59 ml) water
2 eggs
4 tablespoons (56 g) unsalted butter, melted and cooled
1 tablespoon (20 g) honey
1 teaspoon (5 ml) vanilla extract

FOR THE FILLING:

8 ounces (226 g) cream cheese
2 tablespoons (30 ml) grapefruit juice
1 teaspoon (5 ml) orange liqueur
1 teaspoon (5 ml) vanilla extract
½ vanilla bean, halved and scraped
cup (85 g) confectioners' sugar, plus more if needed
2 tablespoons (30 ml) heavy cream, plus more if needed

FOR THE TOPPINGS:

1 grapefruit, peeled and sliced
Whipped cream
Chocolate syrup

TO MAKE THE BATTER:

Whisk together the flour, cardamom, and salt in a small bowl. Combine the milk, water, eggs, butter, honey, and vanilla extract in a blender. Add the flour mixture, and blend until completely smooth. Place the batter in an airtight container, and refrigerate for at least 2 hours.

TO MAKE THE FILLING:

While the batter rests, use a hand mixer or stand mixer fitted with a whisk attachment to whip the cream cheese until smooth in a medium bowl. Add the grapefruit juice, orange liqueur, vanilla extract, and vanilla bean seeds. Mix until combined. Add the confectioners' sugar, and mix well. Slowly add the heavy cream, and mix until smooth. If too thick, add more heavy cream. If too thin, add more confectioners' sugar. Place filling in an airtight container, and refrigerate until you are ready to use.

TO ASSEMBLE:

Remove the batter from the refrigerator, and mix well. Set a large pan over high heat, and coat with cooking spray. Using a ladle, pour ¼ to ½ cup of batter onto the heated pan. Make sure to spread the batter around the pan to make a thin crepe.

Cook the crepe on one side for 3 to 5 minutes or until it begins to brown. Carefully flip and allow it to brown on the other side.

To assemble, place the cooked crepe on a plate, and spread a layer of the cream cheese filling followed by a layer of grapefruit. Top with whipped cream and a small amount of chocolate syrup.

DIFFICULTY: ▬▬ ▬▬ ▬▬ ▬▬ ▬▬

PREP TIME: 30 MINUTES

COOK TIME: 4 TO 6 MINUTES PER BATCH

YIELD: 12 SERVINGS

DIETARY NOTES: VEGAN

JIAN DUI

Chun-Li and I ordered some jian dui at a match. I couldn't help myself and joked about how the buns resembled her oxhorn hairstyle. She chuckled and said Gen made the same joke. I couldn't believe it. Gen? The same assassin who almost killed me? I had no idea Chun-Li was raised by someone so dangerous, but she told me he has a kind heart that he doesn't let other people see.

INGREDIENTS:

1 cup (175 g) glutinous rice flour,
   plus more if needed
¼ cup (50 g) sugar
¼ teaspoon (1 g) baking powder
7 tablespoons (103.5 ml) warm
   water, plus more if needed
½ teaspoon (2.5 ml) sesame oil
7 ounces (200 g) koshian
½ cup (72 g) white sesame seeds
3 tablespoons (27 g) black sesame
   seeds
Peanut oil, for frying

INSTRUCTIONS:

Combine the sweet rice flour, sugar, and baking powder in a medium bowl. Slowly pour in the water, and mix until it all comes together. Add more water if too dry, and add more sweet rice flour if too wet. Add the sesame oil and form into a log. Cut into 12 equal portions, about 30 grams each, and shape them into balls. Place under a moist towel until needed.

Take 1 of the balls and press in the center, large enough to fit about 1 teaspoon of koshian. Seal in the koshian with the dough and shape back into a ball and return under the moist towel. Repeat the process with the remaining balls.

Set up a bowl with a small portion of water. In another bowl, mix together the white and black sesame seeds. Take one of the balls and lightly wet the outside. Place in the bowl with the sesame seeds, and toss until fully coated. Set on a piece of parchment paper, and repeat the process with the remaining balls.

Heat a deep pot with 3 inches of peanut oil over medium-high to 350°F (180°C). Carefully place several of the jian dui in the oil, but do not overcrowd. Fry until golden brown, 4 to 6 minutes. Transfer to a plate covered with paper towels. Repeat in batches with the remaining jian dui.

DIFFICULTY: ▬ ▬ ▬ ▬ ▬

PREP TIME: 45 MINUTES

COOK TIME: 30 MINUTES

YIELD: 4 SERVINGS

DIETARY NOTES: DAIRY-FREE,
EXTREMELY SPICY, PORK

DAN DAN NOODLES

I know the best food stall for dan dan noodles in Tokyo. Dan always said they were the perfect food to help you recover after a bout. But I had to pick them up because he was always too sore to get them himself after our training. Sometimes I wonder who was training whom.

FOR THE PORK:

1 pound (412 g) ground pork

6 garlic cloves, minced

2 teaspoons (20 g) grated fresh ginger

2 tablespoons (30 ml) Shaoxing wine

2 tablespoons (30 ml) soy sauce

½ teaspoon (1 g) black pepper

2 teaspoons (10 ml) canola oil

½ cup (120 g) sui mi ya cai (preserved mustard greens), chopped

FOR THE SAUCE:

1 to 2 teaspoons (1.5 to 3 g) Sichuan peppercorns

2 tablespoons (44 g) tahini

1½ tablespoons (22 ml) soy sauce

½ tablespoon (7 g) sugar

¼ cup to ⅓ cup (59 to 79 ml) chile oil

FOR SERVING:

1 pound (414 g) packaged fresh thin, long noodles

1 cup (237 ml) chicken broth

1 teaspoon (5 ml) canola oil

2 garlic cloves, minced

3 baby bok choy, quartered

3 scallions, chopped

TO MAKE THE PORK:

In a large bowl, combine pork, garlic, ginger, Shaoxing wine, soy sauce, and pepper. Set aside to marinate for 15 minutes.

Heat canola oil in a wok on high. Add the pork, and cook until done, 4 to 5 minutes. Add the chopped sui mi ya cai, and cook for about 1 minute. Remove from the heat.

TO MAKE THE SAUCE:

Place the peppercorns in a small pan over medium high heat. Allow to toast for about 5 minutes. Transfer to a spice grinder (or mortar and pestle), and finely grind.

Combine the tahini, soy sauce, sugar, chile oil, and ground peppercorns. Set aside.

TO ASSEMBLE AND SERVE:

Cook the noodles according to the packaging. Heat the chicken broth and keep warm.

Heat canola oil in a large pan over medium-high. Add the garlic, and cook until just golden brown. Remove garlic from pan, and set aside. In the same pan, sauté the bok choy until lightly seared, about 5 minutes. Add ¼ cup of water, and cover. Cook until the water has evaporated. Remove from heat and set aside.

Place 3 to 4 tablespoons of the sauce in each of 4 bowls. Add the noodles, bok choy, cooked pork, and toasted garlic. Pour ¼ cup of hot chicken broth in each bowl. Finally, top with scallions, and serve. Make sure to mix everything together before digging in.

DIFFICULTY: ▬▬ ▬ ▬ ▬ ▬

PREP TIME: 2 HOURS

REST TIME: 3 TO 24 HOURS

COOK TIME: 30 MINUTES

YIELD: 20 TO 24 TARTS

DIETARY NOTES: DAIRY, VEGETARIAN

DAN TAT

Dan always orders dan tat for dessert when we eat out, but I'm pretty sure he orders it only because it shares his name. I respect that he has an image to keep, but sometimes he takes things a little too far.

For this recipe you'll need fluted tart molds to get the correct shape for the pastry. They're easily found in most kitchen supply stores or online. You can either buy two dozen to make all of the tarts at once, or bake them in batches.

FOR THE FILLING:

1 cup (236 ml) hot water
½ cup (100 g) sugar
1 teaspoon (4 g) salt
3 whole eggs, plus 1 egg yolk
½ cup (118 ml) evaporated milk
1 teaspoon (5 ml) vanilla extract

FOR THE PASTRY DOUGH:

¾ cup (168 g) room temperature
    unsalted butter, plus ½ cup (112 g)
    cold unsalted butter, cubed
2 cups (290 g) all-purpose flour,
    plus more for dusting
½ teaspoon (2 g) salt
1 teaspoon (5 g) sugar
½ cup (118 ml) cold water

Dan once tried improvising the dough. He thought he knew better than the recipe and freestyled it into a real mess. Don't do what Dan does—make sure to take your time, and follow the recipe carefully.

TO MAKE THE FILLING:

Combine the hot water and sugar. Whisk until the sugar has dissolved. Set aside to cool.

Mix in the remaining ingredients. Pass through a mesh strainer a few times to remove any clumps. Store in an airtight container until ready to use. This can be done the night before.

TO MAKE THE PASTRY DOUGH:

Take ¾ cup (168 g) of butter, and cut into equally thick pieces. Arrange the butter in a 4-inch (10-cm) square on top of plastic wrap. Wrap, and make sure it is shaped like a square. Take a rolling pin and smooth the butter into the square shape of the plastic, merging the butter together into a solid piece. Refrigerate for at least 30 minutes.

Combine the flour, salt, and sugar in a medium bowl. Add the cold, cubed butter, and combine using your hands. Work until it resembles coarse meal, leaving some large chunks of butter.

Add three-quarters of the water. If the dough comes together, you do not need to use the remaining water. If the dough is too dry, add 1 tablespoon of water at a time. Combine the mixture until the dough just comes together. Generously flour a work surface and rolling pin. Place the dough on the counter, and lightly knead until the ball is smooth. Wrap in plastic, and refrigerate for 10 minutes.

Once again, generously flour a work surface and rolling pin. Remove the dough from the plastic wrap, and roll out into a slightly larger square than the butter square. Place butter in the center of the dough diagonally, forming a diamond in a square. Fold the corners of the dough over the butter, cover, and seal. Wrap, and refrigerate for 30 minutes.

Remove from the plastic wrap, and transfer to a lightly floured work surface. Press straight down on the dough with the rolling pin to get the butter and dough to compress. Do this several times across the square. Roll into a 16-inch (40-cm) rectangle. Take the bottom edge of the dough, and fold it three-quarters of the way up. Fold the top edge to meet it. Take the new bottom edge, and fold to the new top edge. Turn the dough 90 degrees and lightly tap together with the rolling pin. Wrap in plastic, and refrigerate for 1 hour.

Continued on page 136 . . .

Remove the dough from the plastic wrap, and orient the dough like a closed book. Repeat the previous steps to once again roll out the dough then fold it into a neat package. At this point, the dough can remain in the refrigerator overnight before assembling.

TO ASSEMBLE:

Preheat oven to 400°F (205°C). Place the dough on a floured work surface. Cut in half, place one half on the work surface, and wrap the other in plastic and return to the refrigerator.

Roll out the pastry to ¼-inch (.6-cm) thickness. Cut out the dough with a cookie cutter larger than a 3-inch (7.5-cm) tart mold. Place each piece of dough in a mold. Freeze for 10 minutes. Repeat with the other dough half.

Fill each tart with the filling until just below the top edge. Place in the lower half of the oven, and bake for 15 minutes. Reduce the heat to 350°F (180°C), and bake for an additional 10 minutes, until custard is set.

Turn off the oven, and let the tarts sit in the oven for 10 minutes. Remove and let cool on a rack for another 5 minutes.

DIFFICULTY: ▬ ▬ ▬ ▬ ▬ ▬
PREP TIME: 1 HOUR
COOK TIME: 1 HOUR
YIELD: 4 TO 6 SERVINGS
DIETARY NOTES: DAIRY, VEGETARIAN

PAV BHAJI

I caught up with Dhalsim after an exhibition match and invited him to grab some celebration food. He took me to a noisy market in the area for some curry that looked so good I got through about half of it before realizing he didn't have any food in front of him. Dhalsim just smiled, motioned to some kids cheerfully eating the pav bhaji that he had ordered, and shifted the conversation to other topics.

FOR THE CURRY:

½ head cauliflower, chopped

2 russet potatoes, peeled and chopped

½ cup (75 g) frozen peas

2 Roma tomatoes, chopped

2 cups (473 ml) water

1 tablespoon (17 g) salt

2 tablespoons (28 g) unsalted butter

¼ medium red onion, chopped

½ green bell pepper, chopped

½ serrano pepper, chopped

1 tablespoon (28 g) garlic paste

2 teaspoons (20 g) ginger paste

½ teaspoon (1 g) ground turmeric

¼ teaspoon (.5 g) garam masala

½ tablespoon (3 g) ground coriander

1 tablespoon (7 g) Pav Bhaji Masala (page 27)

Salt

FOR SERVING:

Ladi Pav (page 24)

Unsalted butter

½ medium red onion, chopped

1 bunch fresh cilantro, chopped

2 lemons, halved

TO MAKE THE CURRY:

Put the cauliflower, potatoes, peas, tomatoes, water, and salt in a large pot over medium-high heat, and bring to a boil. Reduce the heat, and simmer until the vegetables have softened, 18 to 25 minutes.

If the pot seems to have too much liquid in it, drain about half the water and set it aside. Mash the vegetables until smooth. If too dry, add back a bit of the water. Transfer to a large bowl.

In the same pot, add butter over medium-high heat. Once melted, add the onion, and cook until softened, about 5 minutes. Add the green pepper and serrano pepper, and cook for another 3 minutes. Add the garlic paste, ginger paste, turmeric, garam masala, ground coriander, and Pav Bhaji Masala. Stir until well combined and fragrant. Add the mashed vegetables, and mix together. If too thick, add more of the reserved water. Taste and season with salt. Keep the bhaji warm until you are ready to serve.

TO ASSEMBLE:

Prepare the Ladi Pav by slicing each in half, 2 buns per serving. Preheat a flat pan over medium-high heat. Butter the insides of each of the Ladi Pav. Place the Ladi Pav buttered side down in the flat pan, and heat until it just starts to brown. Flip and press down. Cook until that side is toasted.

To serve, take 2 ladlefuls of bhaji. Top with butter, red onion, cilantro, and a lemon half. Serve with 2 toasted Ladi Pav buns.

PREP TIME: 15 MINUTES

COOK TIME: 30 MINUTES

YIELD: 2 DRINKS

DIETARY NOTES: GLUTEN-FREE, VEGAN

YOGA SUNBURST

Dhalsim and I shared a delicious order of masala chai. The heat reminded me of the amazing fire breathing I always see him do, so I asked him what the secret behind his flames was. "My beautiful family," he responded without hesitating. "They are the warmth that gives me my strength."

INGREDIENTS:

1 cinnamon stick

3 green cardamom pods

10 black peppercorns

4 whole cloves

2-inch (5-cm) piece fresh ginger, peeled and sliced

2 to 4 tablespoons (28 to 56 g) brown sugar

2 cups (473 ml) water

4 black-tea bags

1½ cups (355 ml) coconut milk

INSTRUCTIONS:

Lightly crush the cinnamon stick, cardamom pods, black peppercorns, and cloves. Transfer to a pot with ginger, brown sugar, and water. Heat over medium-high, and bring a boil. Reduce the heat, and simmer for 15 minutes.

Add the tea bags and coconut milk. Simmer for 5 minutes. Remove from the heat, cover, and let sit for 10 minutes. Strain and serve.

The chai can be cooled and stored in an airtight container in the refrigerator for up to 3 days. To warm up, place in a saucepan and heat for 5 minutes.

DIFFICULTY: ▬ ▬ ▬ ▬ ▬ ▬

PREP TIME: 1 HOUR

COOK TIME: 2 HOURS

YIELD: 4 TO 6 SERVINGS

DIETARY NOTES: DAIRY-FREE

CHANKO NABE

I ran into E. Honda after a match (he's not hard to pick out of a crowd) and wanted to catch up. He brushed aside any suggestions I made, instead insisting I join him and his roommates at their sumo heya for his favorite food, chanko nabe. It's an extremely healthy meal, but there's so much of it, I could barely move after finishing my bowl! When E. Honda was done, though, he thanked me for joining him, then headed out to continue his training. He ate three times as much as I did!

FOR THE BROTH:

4 cups (946 ml) chicken broth

2 cups (473 ml) water

1 sheet kombu

3 scallions, cut into large pieces

½ medium yellow onion, quartered

1 head garlic, halved

2-inch (5-cm) piece fresh ginger, peeled and sliced

3 dried shiitake mushrooms

2 tablespoons (30 ml) sake

FOR THE TSUKUNE:

1 pound ground chicken

1 whole egg, plus 1 egg yolk

2 teaspoons (17 g) ginger paste

1 tablespoon (15 ml) soy sauce
cup (76 g) panko bread crumbs

2 scallions, chopped

FOR THE CHANKO NABE:

1 daikon, peeled and sliced thickly

2 carrots, peeled and cut into bite-size pieces

¼ medium Napa cabbage, sliced thickly

¼ cup (70 g) white miso

2 baby bok choy, quartered

8 ounces (226 g) extra firm tofu, cut into large portions

8 shiitake mushrooms

1 bunch enoki mushrooms

1 bunch shimeji mushrooms

3 scallions, cut into 3-inch pieces

2 packages frozen udon noodles

TO MAKE THE BROTH:

Combine all ingredients in a large pot over medium-high heat. Bring to a boil, then reduce the heat and simmer for an hour. Strain and set aside.

TO MAKE THE TSUKUNE:

Combine all the ingredients until the mixture just comes together. Split and shape into equal-size meatballs. Set aside.

TO MAKE THE CHANKO NABE:

Prepare a large pot by placing the daikon and carrots at the bottom. Top with Napa cabbage. Place the miso in the center. Surround the miso with the bok choy, tofu, shiitake mushrooms, and tsukune.

Pour in the broth, and cover everything most of the way. Set over medium-high heat until it is just about to boil. Reduce the heat, and simmer until the meatballs are cooked through, about 10 minutes.

Add the enoki mushrooms, shimeji mushrooms, scallions, and udon. Heat until the udon is cooked through. Serve hot.

DIFFICULTY: ▬ ▬ ▭ ▭ ▭

PREP TIME: 1 HOUR

REST TIME: 2 HOURS

COOK TIME: 15 TO 20 MINUTES

YIELD: 12 BUNS

DIETARY NOTES: DAIRY

BO LO BAO

I am such a big fan of Fei Long's kung fu movies. I almost broke our TV imitating his moves when I was younger. I was so thrilled to get a chance to sit down with him in Hong Kong for some delicious bo lo bao, but I was too starstruck to remember any of the conversation. Argh, what did we talk about? Did I just talk about his movies the whole time?

FOR THE TOPPING:

1 cup (140 g) all-purpose flour

¾ teaspoon (3 g) baking powder

½ teaspoon (2 g) baking soda

Pinch of salt

¼ cup plus 1 tablespoon (70 g) unsalted butter, divided

½ cup (100 g) sugar

1 egg yolk

½ teaspoon (2.5 g) vanilla extract

1 tablespoon (15 ml) milk

FOR THE BUN:

1½ cups plus 3 tablespoons (283 g) bread flour, divided

⅓ cup (79 ml) cold milk, plus ½ cup (118 ml) warm milk, heated to 100°F to 110°F (37°C to 43°C), plus more if needed

2 teaspoons (7 g) active dry yeast

1 cup (140 g) all-purpose flour, plus more if needed

2 teaspoons (7 g) salt

¼ cup (50 g) sugar

⅓ cup (79 ml) sweetened condensed milk

1 egg

1 teaspoon (5 ml) vanilla extract

3 tablespoons (42 g) unsalted butter, softened

Neutral oil or nonstick spray, for oiling

FOR THE EGG WASH:

1 egg

1 tablespoon (15 ml) milk

1 teaspoon (5 g) sugar

TO MAKE THE TOPPING:

Combine the flour, baking powder, baking soda, and salt in a small bowl. In large bowl using an electric hand mixer or a whisk, cream the butter until smooth. Add the sugar, and mix until fluffy. Add the egg yolk, vanilla extract, and milk, and mix until well combined. Add the flour mixture, and mix until just combined. Transfer to plastic wrap, and create a log. Wrap and refrigerate for 1 hour or until firm.

TO MAKE THE BUN:

Combine 3 tablespoons (33 g) bread flour and ⅓ cup (79 ml) cold milk in a saucepan over medium-high heat to create tangzhong. Whisk until it comes together, about 1 minute. Set aside to cool.

Combine the yeast and warm milk in a small bowl, and let rest for 5 minutes, allowing the yeast to become active and frothy.

Combine the remaining bread flour, all-purpose flour, salt, and sugar in a large bowl of a stand mixer fitted with a dough hook. Add the tangzhong, yeast mixture, sweetened condensed milk, and egg to the bowl, and mix on medium speed until it just comes together.

While the dough begins to form, add the butter 1 tablespoon at a time. Knead the dough for 5 minutes. If the dough is too sticky, add 1 tablespoon of flour at a time. If it is too dry, add 1 tablespoon of milk at a time. Transfer to an oiled bowl, cover, and let rest for 1 hour or until dough has doubled in size.

Once doubled, punch down and knead for a few minutes, then split the dough into 12 equal portions (60 g) and form into round balls. Cover and allow to rise again for 30 minutes, or until it doubles in size. Preheat oven to 350°F (180°C).

Continued on page 146 . . .

TO ASSEMBLE:

Take the topping, and cut the log into 12 equal portions. If the dough is too hard to cut, allow to warm up at room temperature until you can easily cut it. Take one of the discs and place it between 2 pieces of parchment paper. Carefully roll out the disc until it is about 2½ inches in diameter. Make sure not to put too much pressure or the dough might crack and split in the center. It's okay if the edges split.

Gently place the discs on each of the buns, and lightly press the sides on. It shouldn't completely cover the bun.

TO MAKE THE EGG WASH:

Combine the egg yolk, milk, and sugar, and whisk until combined. Brush each of the buns with the egg wash. Let sit for 2 to 3 minutes to let the wash dry slightly. Brush with another layer of egg wash. Bake for 15 to 18 minutes until golden brown.

DIFFICULTY:

PREP TIME: 2 HOURS

REST TIME: 10 HOURS

COOK TIME: 1½ HOURS

YIELD: 16 BUNS

DIETARY NOTES: DAIRY-FREE, PORK

CHAR SIU BAOZI

The last time I had some char siu baozi, I was sharing an order with Chun-Li. She said they always reminded her of Gen because it's one of his favorite snacks. I remember sparring with Gen in the past, but I couldn't imagine sharing a meal with him. I told Chun-Li as much, and she agreed. He's not the same person she remembers training under.

FOR THE DOUGH:

1½ teaspoons (5 g) active dry yeast

¾ cup (177 ml) warm water, heated to 100°F to 110°F (37°C to 43°C)

¼ cup (59 ml) canola oil, plus more for bowl

2¼ cups (350 g) all-purpose flour

¾ cup (130 g) cornstarch

2 teaspoons (9 g) baking powder

¼ cup (50 g) sugar

2 teaspoons (7 g) salt

FOR THE CHAR SIU:

2 tablespoons (30 g) brown sugar

1 teaspoon (1 g) Chinese five-spice powder

1 teaspoon (3 g) salt

½ teaspoon (.5 g) black pepper

2 garlic cloves, minced

2 tablespoons (30 ml) Shaoxing wine

1 tablespoon (15 ml) soy sauce

1 tablespoon (15 ml) hoisin sauce

1 teaspoon (5 ml) sesame oil

¼ teaspoon (1.5 ml) red food dye (optional)

2 pounds (907 g) pork shoulder

3 tablespoons (60 g) honey

FOR THE FILLING:

2 teaspoons (8 g) sugar

1 tablespoon (20 g) honey

2 tablespoons (32 g) oyster sauce

1 tablespoon (15 ml) soy sauce

1 teaspoon (5 ml) sesame oil

½ cup (118 ml) chicken stock

2 teaspoons (10 ml) canola oil

3 shallots, chopped

1 tablespoon (10 g) cornstarch

1½ pounds (680 g) Char Siu, chopped

TO MAKE THE DOUGH:

Mix the yeast, water, and canola oil in a small bowl, and let rest for 5 minutes, allowing the yeast to become active and frothy.

Combine the flour, cornstarch, baking powder, sugar, and salt in a large bowl. Slowly mix in the liquid with the flour until it all comes together. Transfer to a lightly floured work surface, and knead for 5 minutes. Place the dough in an oiled bowl, and cover. Let it rest until it doubles in size, about 2 hours.

TO MAKE THE CHAR SIU:

Combine the brown sugar, five-spice powder, salt, pepper, garlic, wine, soy sauce, hoisin sauce, sesame oil, and food dye in a small bowl. Remove 2½ tablespoons (22.5 ml) of the marinade, and place in an airtight container. Store in the refrigerator.

Cut the pork into equal portions, about 3 inches thick, and leave the excess fat on the pork. Place in a deep baking tray, and rub with the remaining marinade, making sure all parts are covered. Cover the pan, and refrigerate overnight, at least 8 hours.

Preheat oven to 425°F (220°C). Line a baking tray with aluminum foil, and top with a metal rack. Place the pork on the rack, and fill the bottom of the pan with about 1 cup of water. Roast for 20 minutes. Flip, and roast for another 10 to 20 minutes, until the pork registers at 145°F (63°C). If all the water has evaporated, add more to keep the bottom of the pan from smoking.

While the pork is roasting, take the reserved marinade and mix with the honey. Baste the pork with about half the mixture, and roast for another 5 minutes. Flip, baste with the remaining sauce, and cook for another 5 minutes. If it hasn't caramelized, turn on the broiler, and cook until it just crisps up. Cover in aluminum foil, and let rest for 15 minutes before cutting.

Continued on page 150 . . .

TO MAKE THE FILLING:

Combine the sugar, honey, oyster sauce, soy sauce, sesame oil, and chicken stock in a small bowl. Heat a pan over medium-high heat. Add canola oil, and cook the shallots until softened, about 5 minutes. Reduce the heat to medium-low, and add the liquid mixture to the pan. Cook, and bring to a light simmer.

Combine cornstarch and about 2 tablespoons of water in a small bowl. Add to the pan, and whisk until it starts to thicken. Take off the heat, and mix into the pork. Set aside.

TO ASSEMBLE:

Punch down the dough and roll out into a long tube. Split into 16 equal pieces, and form into balls. Take a portion and roll out to about 5 inches wide. When rolling out, make sure not to make the center too thin. Add some of the filling in the center of the dough. Pleat the bun until sealed. Place the bun on a piece of parchment paper. Repeat with the remaining portions. Place water in a pot with a steamer basket, and bring to a boil. Place 4 to 6 bao in the basket with the parchment. Place over the boiling water, cover, and let steam for 12 to 15 minutes.

DIFFICULTY:

PREP TIME: 45 MINUTES

COOK TIME: 15 MINUTES

YIELD: 4 SKEWERS

DIETARY NOTES: VEGAN

DANGO

It was a lot of fun talking to Gouken about Ryu and Ken. He had so many good stories to share about their training. Between big bites of dango, he had a few choice words about Dan's lack of discipline and his poor excuse of a fighting style. I joked that he should take me in as a pupil as well, but he very quickly rejected the idea.

FOR THE DANGO:

¾ cup (120 g) joshinko rice flour

⅓ cup plus 1 tablespoon (50 g)
   shiratamako rice flour

½ tablespoon (6.5 g) sugar

1 teaspoon (2.5 g) matcha

½ cup (118 ml) hot water

FOR THE MITARASHI SYRUP:

2 tablespoons (26 g) sugar

1 tablespoon (14 g) brown sugar

1¼ tablespoons (19 ml) soy sauce

1 tablespoon (15 ml) mirin

½ cup (118 ml) plus 1 tablespoon
   (15 ml) water

1 tablespoon (12 g) potato starch

It may seem tempting to use different types of rice flour as substitutions for the joshinko and shiratamako rice flour, but I just can't recommend it! To get the right texture, I do recommend making a trip to your local Japanese market or perhaps looking online.

TO MAKE THE DANGO:

Combine the joshinko, shiratamako, sugar, and matcha in a medium bowl. Slowly begin to pour in the ½ cup (118 ml) water, and stir. You may need more or less water. The consistency of the dough should feel like an earlobe. Lightly knead the dough until completely smooth. Divide the dough into 12 equal pieces. With your hands lightly moistened, shape the dough into smooth balls. Transfer to a plate, and cover with a moist towel to keep the dough from drying out.

Bring a pot with water to a boil. Add the dango to the pot. Give them a stir so they don't stick to the bottom. Once the dumplings start to float, they are done, 3 to 4 minutes. Transfer to a bowl with ice water. Let rest for about 2 minutes

Drain the dango, and transfer to a baking pan that has been lightly moistened with water. Skewer 3 dango on a bamboo skewer, set on the baking sheet, and cover with a damp towel to keep the dango from drying out. Repeat with remaining dango.

TO MAKE THE MITARASHI SYRUP:

Combine the sugar, brown sugar, soy sauce, mirin, and water in a small saucepan over medium-high heat until the sugar has dissolved.

Combine the potato starch and 1 tablespoon (15 ml) of water in a small bowl. Add the potato starch slurry to the saucepan. Stir until the sauce thickens. Take off the heat, and set aside until you are ready to serve.

Heat a frying pan over medium, and place the skewered dango on the pan. Cook until each side is nicely browned, about 2 minutes per side. Top with mitarashi syrup.

DIFFICULTY:
PREP TIME: 25 MINUTES
COOK TIME: 15 MINUTES
YIELD: 2 SERVINGS
DIETARY NOTES: DAIRY-FREE

SALMON OCHAZUKE

Rashid told me that Guy was writing a blog on his teachings of Bushinryu, so I messaged him and scheduled lunch with him when I was in Metro City. He took me to the only place he knew in the city that served his favorite dish, salmon ochazuke. It was pretty mild for a salmon dish, but the taste was a really unique blend of fish and tea. He said the meal helps center him for his training, but I just enjoyed the food.

INGREDIENTS:

¼ pound (113 g) salmon, cut into 2 pieces

Salt

Black pepper

2 teaspoons (10 ml) canola oil

1 cup (370 g) cooked rice

½ teaspoon (3 g) sesame seeds

1 scallion, green part only, finely minced

2 teaspoons (1 g) shredded nori

1 tablespoon (10 g) bubu arare (rice crackers), crushed

1 tablespoon (5 g) hojicha or other green tea leaves

1½ cup (118 ml) hot water

1 teaspoon (5 ml) soy sauce

Wasabi, prepared (optional)

INSTRUCTIONS:

Generously season the salmon with salt and pepper on all sides. Place a medium-size pan over medium-high heat and add canola oil. Place the salmon in the pan skin side down, and cook until the skin crisps up, about 4 minutes.

Flip the salmon, and cook for another 2 minutes, or until it browns slightly. Flip the salmon on its side, and cook until it browns, about 1 minute. Flip to the other side, and cook until it browns, about 1 minute. Place the salmon on a plate, and allow to cool. Remove the skin and discard. Shred the salmon.

Split the cooked rice between 2 bowls. Top with the salmon, sesame seeds, scallions, nori, and crushed bubu arare.

Combine the hojicha and hot water, and steep for 3 minutes. Remove the leaves, and mix in the soy sauce. If using wasabi, place a small dollop on top of the portion. Pour the tea evenly between the 2 bowls, and enjoy.

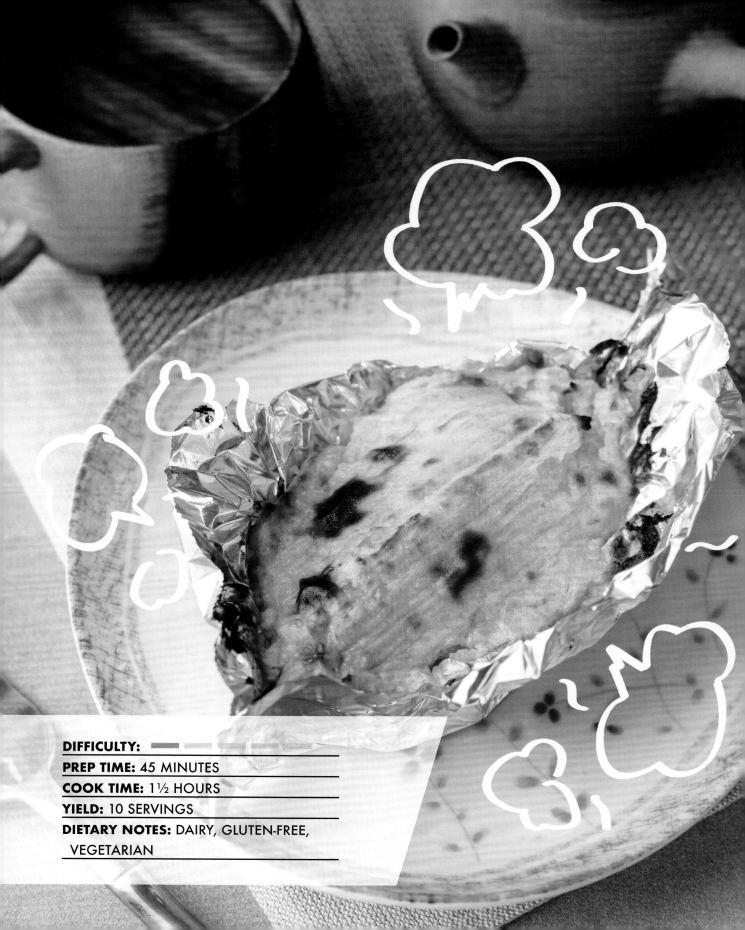

DIFFICULTY: ▬▬ ▬ ▬

PREP TIME: 45 MINUTES

COOK TIME: 1½ HOURS

YIELD: 10 SERVINGS

DIETARY NOTES: DAIRY, GLUTEN-FREE, VEGETARIAN

ROAST SWEET POTATO

I asked Ibuki if she had any street food suggestions for my trip. I assumed she'd want to go to an ice cream place like she always does, but I was shocked when she showed me this cute food cart selling roast sweet potatoes. They were so delicious that I ordered seconds.

INGREDIENTS:

3 (about 1.7 kg) Japanese sweet potatoes

3 tablespoons (42 g) unsalted butter

⅓ cup (67 g) sugar

3 tablespoons (50 g) honey

1 whole egg plus 1 egg yolk

¼ cup (60 ml) plus 1 tablespoon (15 ml) heavy cream, divided, plus more if needed

1½ teaspoon (7.5 ml) vanilla extract

¼ teaspoon (1.25 ml) almond extract

INSTRUCTIONS:

Preheat oven to 400°F (205°C). Poke several holes into the sweet potatoes with a fork. Lightly wrap in aluminum foil, leaving small holes for steam to escape. Bake for 1 hour or until soft and cooked through. Set aside until cool enough to work with. Reduce the oven to 350°F (180°C).

Cut the potatoes in half. Scoop the insides into a medium bowl, and discard the skins.

Place the butter in a pot over medium heat, and cook until melted. Add the potatoes, sugar, and honey, and mash until smooth. Turn down the heat to low. Add the egg yolk, and whisk so the egg doesn't scramble. Continue whisking while slowly adding the ¼ cup heavy cream. Mix until well combined. If the mixture is not smooth, add more heavy cream, one tablespoon (15 ml) at a time.

Remove from the heat. Mix in the vanilla and almond extracts. Divide into 10 portions. Shape 10 pieces of aluminum foil into bowls that are roughly sweet potato shaped. Add the sweet potato portions in each of the foil molds and smooth the top.

Prepare an egg wash by combining the whole egg and remaining 1 tablespoon heavy cream, and brush each of the sweet potato portions. Bake for 15 minutes. Turn on the broiler, and broil until the tops start to brown.

DIFFICULTY: ▬
PREP TIME: 30 MINUTES
COOK TIME: 30 MINUTES
YIELD: 4 SERVINGS
DIETARY NOTES: DAIRY, EXTREMELY SPICY

TTEOKBOKKI

Juri has always given me mixed signals, but I was surprised when she accepted my offer to grab some food. Since a super popular Korean market was nearby, we walked over to a street vendor where Juri ordered me something called tteokbokki. She didn't tell me how spicy it was, but Juri was both surprised and impressed that I finished the whole thing. My mouth was an inferno, but I didn't want to look weak in front of Juri so I played it off.

This recipe calls for a lot of special ingredients including gochujang, which I've mentioned before. You'll also need red pepper flakes known as gochugaru and jocheong, which is a rice syrup you can find in Korean markets or online. You can substitute honey for jocheong, but the flavor is completely different.

FOR THE SAUCE:

3 tablespoons (36 g) gochujang

2 tablespoons (24 g) gochugaru

1 tablespoon (13 g) sugar

2 tablespoons (40 g) jocheong

1 tablespoon (15 ml) soy sauce

3 garlic cloves, minced

1 tablespoon (24 g) ginger paste
   or puree

FOR THE TTEOKBOKKI:

3 cups (710 ml) Korean dashi stock
   or vegetable stock

1 pound (907 g) cylindrical rice cakes

4 scallions, large slices

2 sheets fried fish cake, cut into bite-
   size pieces

8 ounces (227 g) mozzarella,
   shredded (optional)

TO MAKE THE SAUCE:

In a small bowl, combine all ingredients. Set aside.

TO MAKE THE TTEOKBOKKI:

In a large, oven-safe pan, add the stock and the mixed sauce, and stir together. Place over medium-high heat, and bring to a boil. Add the rice cakes, and mix in well. Let cook until the rice cakes become soft, about 8 minutes. Add the scallions and fish cakes, and cook until the fish cakes heat up, about 3 minutes.

If adding cheese, top with mozzarella and place under a broiler. Cook until the cheese has melted and is starting to brown a bit.

Fried fish cakes can be found in most Asian grocery stores in a variety of shapes, both frozen or fresh.

If your rice cakes are dried and not fresh, soak them in water for at least 20 minutes before starting this recipe to soften them.

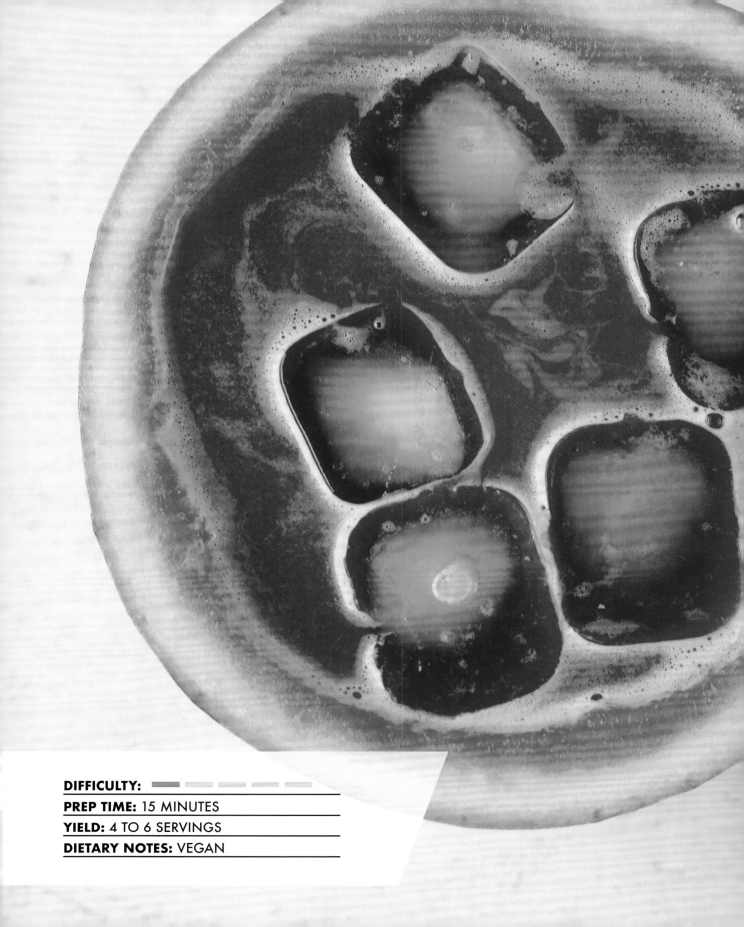

DIFFICULTY:
PREP TIME: 15 MINUTES
YIELD: 4 TO 6 SERVINGS
DIETARY NOTES: VEGAN

FUHARENKYAKU

Juri definitely looked at me differently after all that spicy food. She ordered soju in watermelon halves for the table to "celebrate finding someone who can actually handle some heat." With how ferociously I've seen her fight in the ring, I suspect she's too hot to handle for most of her opponents.

INGREDIENTS:

1 small watermelon
2 cups (473 ml) soju
1½ cups (355 ml) club soda
Ice

INSTRUCTIONS:

Cut a watermelon in half, scoop out the interior, and transfer it to a blender. Reserve the rind. Blend the fruit until smooth. Pour through a fine mesh strainer into a pitcher. Add the soju, and mix together. Refrigerate until ready to serve.

When serving, add the club soda and ice. One super move I recommend is to serve the drink in the hollowed-out watermelon.

DIFFICULTY: ▬ ▬ ▬ ▬ ▬

PREP TIME: 45 MINUTES

COOK TIME: 30 MINUTES

YIELD: 12 SERVINGS

DIETARY NOTES: DAIRY

CORN DOG

Karin hosted one of her fancy house parties before we left for the tournament. She's not big on street food, but I couldn't help myself and brought corn dogs from a stall on my way over. You wouldn't believe the look of disgust on her face when she saw them set out among all the expensive food.

INGREDIENTS: ⓘ

12 wooden skewers

8 hot dogs, cut in thirds

6 mozzarella sticks, halved

2 cups (319 g) all-purpose flour, divided

1 teaspoon (1 g) ichimi togarashi

1½ tablespoons (19 g) sugar

1 teaspoon (4 g) salt

1 tablespoon (13 g) baking powder

1 cup (237 ml) milk

2 eggs

Peanut oil, for frying

2 cups (110 g) panko bread crumbs

¼ cup (50 g) sugar

INSTRUCTIONS:

Take a wooden skewer, and place a third of a hot dog, followed by a half piece of mozzarella, and another hot dog portion. Repeat with the remaining skewers. Place in the refrigerator until you are ready to batter them.

In a medium bowl, combine 1¾ cups (285 g) flour, ichimi togarashi, sugar, salt, and baking powder.

In a small bowl, whisk the milk and eggs together.

Add milk and egg mixture to the dry ingredients, and whisk until the batter comes together; it should be pretty thick. Transfer to a tall glass; this will make it easier to cover the skewers in batter later, but be sure to leave 1 or 2 inches of space at the top of the glass. Refrigerate until you are ready to use.

Fill a deep pot with 2 inches of peanut oil, and place over medium heat to 350°F (180°C). Set the cup with batter and 2 shallow dishes nearby to create an assembly line. Fill one dish with the remaining ¼ cup (34 g) of flour and the second with the panko bread crumbs.

First, take a few prepared skewers and roll them in the flour. Next, dip the skewers in the batter-filled glass. You will need to dip them several times in the batter to be sure the hot dog and cheese are completely covered. Then roll the batter-covered skewers in panko bread crumbs. Carefully place 2 to 3 skewers in the oil and allow to fry until golden brown. Transfer to a wire rack and let any excess oil drain. Repeat with the remaining skewers.

Roll each of the corn dogs in the sugar, and serve with your favorite condiments.

Feel free to split these up however you like. If you want more cheese, just use more cheese sticks!

DIFFICULTY:

PREP TIME: 45 MINUTES

COOK TIME: 45 MINUTES

YIELD: 3 SERVINGS

DIETARY NOTES: DAIRY-FREE, GLUTEN-FREE

CHIRASHI

Karin's culinary contribution to her party was a heaping bowl of chirashi with the highest-grade fish around. It's very straightforward (like Karin) but requires a lot of expense and extravagance (also very Karin). I told her I didn't think the fish paired well with the corn dogs I brought, but she didn't appreciate the joke enough to offer a retort.

INGREDIENTS:

2 cups cooked Sushi Rice (page 27)

1 tablespoon (9 g) sesame seeds

4 ounces (115 g) sushi-grade raw tuna, thinly sliced

4 ounces (115 g) sushi-grade raw salmon, thinly sliced

2 ounces (56 g) sushi-grade raw hamachi (yellowtail), thinly sliced

4 ounces (115 g) sushi-grade raw ikura (salmon roe)

½ small cucumber, thinly sliced

½ medium avocado, thinly sliced

1 scallion, finely diced

½ cup (90 g) shelled edamame

2 tablespoons (1½ g) shredded nori

2 teaspoons (34 g) pickled ginger

Wasabi, prepared, for topping

INSTRUCTIONS:

Split the rice among 3 serving bowls. Sprinkle with sesame seeds. Top with the tuna, salmon, hamachi, ikura, cucumbers, avocado, scallion, and edamame. Place a portion of nori, pickled ginger, and wasabi on top, and serve.

DIFFICULTY: ▬ ▬ ▭ ▭ ▭

PREP TIME: 1 HOUR

COOK TIME: 30 MINUTES

YIELD: 16 ROLLS

DIETARY NOTES: DAIRY-FREE

GỎI CUỐN

One of the stops on the tournament took me to a tranquil coastal arena in Vietnam. I heard rumors from the crowd of some shady business with M. Bison in the past, so on a whim, I decided to play detective and ask around for clues. I got maybe 10 minutes into my search before I was stopped in my tracks by of a food cart with amazing-looking spring rolls. I loved them so much, the peanut sauce playing perfectly with the herbs and shrimp, that I forgot I was investigating and headed back to the arena with nothing to show for it.

FOR THE NƯỚC CHẤM:

⅓ cup (85 g) water

¼ cup (50 g) sugar

¼ cup (77 g) fish sauce

2 tablespoons (35 g) lime juice

1 Thai chile, sliced

4 garlic cloves, minced

FOR THE PEANUT SAUCE:

¼ cup (90 g) smooth peanut butter

1 tablespoon (15 ml) rice vinegar

2 tablespoons (30 ml) coconut milk

1 tablespoon (22 g) honey

1 teaspoon (5 ml) sesame oil

FOR THE GỎI CUỐN:

16 ounces (375 g) firm tofu

1 teaspoon (10 ml) canola oil

24 jumbo or large shrimp, shelled and cleaned

½ cup (118 ml) water, plus more warm water for assembly

16 round rice paper sheets

1 head butter lettuce

8 ounces (227 g) rice vermicelli, cooked

1 cucumber, peeled and cut into long slices

2 carrots, peeled and julienned

⅓ cup fresh cilantro

⅓ cup fresh mint

⅓ cup fresh Thai basil

TO MAKE THE NƯỚC CHẤM:

Combine all the ingredients in a small bowl, and whisk together until the sugar has dissolved. Store in an airtight container in the refrigerator for up to 2 weeks.

TO MAKE THE PEANUT SAUCE:

Combine all the ingredients in a small bowl. Serve immediately, or store in the refrigerator until you are ready to serve. The sauce will thicken in the refrigerator slightly.

TO MAKE THE GỎI CUỐN:

Place the tofu between 2 plates and top with a heavy object. Allow to rest for 5 minutes in order to remove excess liquid. Cut the tofu into 16 rectangle pieces, and set aside.

Place a pan with oil over medium-high heat. Add the tofu, and cook until all sides have slightly browned. Transfer to a plate.

Place the shrimp and water in a pan over medium-high heat. Cover, and bring to a boil for 2 minutes or until the shrimp is cooked. Remove shrimp from the pan and allow to cool for 5 minutes. Cut the shrimp in half, and set aside.

Fill a deep dish with lukewarm water. Soak a rice paper sheet in the dish until it softens slightly. Place on a cutting board. Place a piece of butter lettuce in the lower half of the rice paper sheet. Add a portion of vermicelli, 1 piece of tofu, 2 to 3 slices of cucumber, a small portion of carrots, and the herbs on top of the butter lettuce. Place three pieces of shrimp a half inch to an inch above the other ingredients, making sure the orange part of the halved shrimp is facing down. Grab the lower edge of the rice paper and start rolling the lettuce portion. When you reach the shrimp, tuck the sides in. Continuing rolling the shrimp until sealed. Repeat until all ingredients have been used, then serve rolls with both sauces.

DIFFICULTY: — — — — — — — —

PREP TIME: 10 MINUTES

YIELD: 2 DRINKS

DIETARY NOTES: VEGAN

PSYCHO BLAST

I thought about what kind of drink M. Bison would partake in, if he even enjoys anything, and I came up empty at first. The few times I've had to face him in a fight were terrible experiences, and I almost felt intoxicated going up against his Psycho Power. That's how I came up with this drink, a deep purple punch in the gut. But it's also a bit sweet, because between you and me, I love sweeter drinks!

INGREDIENTS:

2 ounces (60 ml) vodka
1 ounce (30 ml) blue curaçao
1 ounce (30 ml) grenadine
2 ounces (60 ml) raspberry liqueur
2 ounces (60 ml) apple juice
½ ounce (15 ml) lime juice
Ice

INSTRUCTIONS:

Combine all ingredients in a cocktail shaker. Cover and shake for 10 seconds. Strain between 2 glasses with ice.

DIFFICULTY: ▬▬ ▬ ▬ ▬ ▬

PREP TIME: 15 MINUTES

COOK TIME: 10 MINUTES

YIELD: 2 DRINKS

DIETARY NOTES: DAIRY, VEGETARIAN

TENGU DAOSHI

I had a fun friendly duel with Maki, but I was distracted by how impressive her tonfa skills were and got a big bruise on my arm. She felt bad about it, so she picked up some taro tea from a nearby vendor to ice the bruise, but it was so tasty I ended up drinking it all before the cold did anything.

INGREDIENTS:

5 cups (1183 ml) water, plus ½ cup (118 ml) hot water

½ cup (90 g) instant black tapioca pearls

2 tablespoons (44 g) honey

2 tablespoons (28 g) brown sugar

2½ cups (592 ml) cold green tea

¼ cup (50 g) taro powder

½ cup (118 ml) coconut milk

2 tablespoons (30 ml) sweetened condensed milk

7 ice cubes

INSTRUCTIONS:

Place a medium saucepan filled with the 5 cups of water over medium-high heat. Bring to a boil, and add the instant black tapioca pearls. Stir and cook for 2 to 3 minutes or until the pearls float. Cover, and reduce the heat to medium-low, continuing to cook for another 2 to 3 minutes. Turn off the heat and keep covered for another 2 to 4 minutes or until the tapioca has softened completely. Drain through a strainer, and rinse thoroughly with cold water.

Combine honey, sugar, and the ½ cup (118 ml) of hot water in a medium bowl. Whisk together until the sugar has dissolved. Add the tapioca, and allow to rest for 10 minutes. Refrigerate for up to 6 hours, but to serve immediately, divide the boba between 2 large glasses.

Combine the green tea, taro powder, coconut milk, and sweetened condensed milk in a blender. Blend until combined. Add the ice cubes and blend until crushed. Pour in the 2 glasses with the boba. Enjoy with a large straw.

Maki adds boba to every drink. She can't get enough of the stuff!

DIFFICULTY: ▬ ▬ ▬ ▬ ▬ ▬

PREP TIME: 30 MINUTES

COOK TIME: 1 MINUTE

YIELD: 3 SERVINGS

DIETARY NOTES: DAIRY-FREE

KATSUO NO TATAKI

Makoto was too busy to attend the local tournament stop, so I paid her dojo in Tosa a visit. She met up with me at an izakaya where they served an amazing katsuo no tataki, beautiful bonito seared on the sides but raw in the middle. I was initially concerned by her absence from the tournament; the Makoto I know would never pass up a fight. But she told me she had been too busy with renovations and new students to make the trip and was super optimistic about her dojo's future.

FOR THE SAUCE:

¼ cup (59 ml) soy sauce

2 tablespoons (30 ml) rice vinegar

2 tablespoons (30 ml) lemon juice

1 tablespoon (15 ml) yuzu juice

1 tablespoon (16 g) grated fresh ginger

FOR THE FISH:

½ pound (227 g) sushi-grade bonito fillet, skin on

3 shiso leaves, stem removed

½ medium yellow onion, thinly sliced

1 garlic clove, thinly sliced

2 scallions, chopped

TO MAKE THE SAUCE:

Combine all the ingredients for the sauce and set aside.

TO MAKE THE FISH:

Gently rinse the bonito, and pat dry. If using a kitchen torch, place on a heat-safe wire rack in a baking sheet. Lightly brown the outside of the fillet. If using a nonstick pan, heat over medium-high. Lightly sear for about 10 to 15 seconds per side. Transfer to an ice bath for up to 15 minutes.

Meanwhile, prepare 3 plates by placing the shiso leaves on the bottom, top with the sliced onions, and set aside.

Once the fish has cooled, remove from the ice bath, and pat dry. Slice the bonito into 3 half-inch-thick slices. Arrange on top of the onions. Top with the sliced garlic and scallions. Pour about half the sauce on top. Transfer the remaining sauce to a small plate, and serve.

DIFFICULTY: ▬ ▬ ▬ ▬ ▬

PREP TIME: 2 HOURS

REST TIME: 24 HOURS

COOK TIME: 1½ HOURS

YIELD: 16 BUNS

DIETARY NOTES: VEGETARIAN

KARE PAN

I had a hankering for some kare pan the other day, so I grabbed some from a convenience store. I was so distracted by the gorgeous fried crunch that I almost ran face first into an elderly gentleman holding what I think was a pet turtle. I apologized, but he introduced himself as Oro and told me he didn't mind getting run over by such a beautiful young woman like myself. I laughed nervously, then very quickly walked away.

FOR THE ROUX: (!)

¼ cup (36 g) all-purpose flour
1 tablespoon (6 g) garam masala
1 teaspoon (1 g) ground turmeric
½ teaspoon (.5 g) ground coriander
½ teaspoon (.5 g) ground fennel
¼ teaspoon (.25 g) ground cinnamon
2 tablespoons (30 g) unsalted butter
1 tablespoon (15 g) tomato paste
1½ tablespoons (22 ml) tonkatsu
   sauce
1 tablespoon (20 g) honey

FOR THE FILLING:

1 tablespoon (15 ml) canola oil
½ medium yellow onion, chopped
4 shiitake mushrooms, chopped
1½ cup (355 ml) vegetable broth
2 medium russet potatoes, peeled
   and cubed
2 carrots, cubed
Salt
Black pepper

FOR THE DOUGH:

2½ cups (380 g) bread flour
½ cup (70 g) cake flour
1 teaspoon (2 g) ground turmeric
1 teaspoon (4 g) salt
1 cup (237 ml) milk
3 tablespoons (42 g) unsalted butter
1 tablespoon (13 g) sugar
2 teaspoons (7 g) active dry yeast
Neutral oil or nonstick spray, for oiling

FOR FRYING:

Peanut oil
2 eggs
2 cups (140 g) panko bread crumbs

TO MAKE THE ROUX:

Combine the flour, garam masala, turmeric, coriander, fennel, and cinnamon in a small bowl. Melt the butter in a small saucepan over medium-high heat. Add the flour and spices to the melted butter. Mix until the flour has absorbed all the butter. Mix in the tomato paste, tonkatsu sauce, and honey. Once combined, turn off the heat, and set the roux aside.

TO MAKE THE FILLING:

Heat a large pot with canola oil over medium-high heat. Add the onions and mushrooms. Cook until softened, about 5 minutes. Add the vegetable broth, potatoes, and carrots. Bring to a boil, then reduce the heat to a simmer. Place the lid slightly ajar, and simmer for 10 to 15 minutes, until potatoes start to get soft. Take a small portion of the roux and place it in a ladle. Place the ladle in the liquid of the pot and slowly mix in. Repeat in small portions until all the roux is added to the pot. Let simmer for 5 minutes or until it thickens. Season with salt and pepper to taste. Allow to cool. Refrigerate overnight.

TO MAKE THE DOUGH:

Combine the bread flour, cake flour, turmeric, and salt in a large bowl. Combine the milk, butter, and sugar in a small saucepan. Place over medium-high heat and cook until the butter just melts. Remove from the heat and allow to cool to 105°F (40.5°C). Add yeast, and let rest for 5 minutes, allowing the yeast to become active and frothy.

Add the milk mixture to the large bowl with the flour, and mix until it just comes together. Knead the dough for 8 minutes. Shape into a ball. Transfer to an oiled bowl, cover, and let rest at room temperature for 1 hour or until it has doubled in size.

(!)

If you can't make your own roux, prepackaged roux (often sold as instant curry sauce mix) works in a pinch. The amount you'll need depends on the brand.

Continued on page 176 . . .

Punch the dough down and lightly knead. Divide the dough into 16 equal portions and shape into balls. To assemble, take a dough portion and roll out to a 4½-inch (11.5-cm) circle. Place a portion of filling, about 1½ to 2 tablespoons (roughly 25 to 30 g), in the center without overfilling the dough. Tightly pinch the edges together until completely sealed. Place the prepared bun on a baking sheet seam side down. Repeat with the remaining dough. Cover with a kitchen towel and let rest for 30 minutes.

Fill a deep pot with 2 inches of peanut oil, and set over medium heat until it reaches 330°F (166°C). Prepare 2 stations for breading the buns. The first station is a bowl with the eggs lightly beaten, and the other station is a plate of panko. Coat each of the buns in the egg and then the panko. Return to the baking tray until the oil has heated up.

Place the buns in the oil, making sure not to overcrowd, and cook for 3 minutes. Flip, then cook for another 3 minutes. Remove the buns from the oil and place onto a plate covered with a paper towel. Repeat these steps with the remaining buns. The oil temperature might drop between each fry, so be sure to let the oil heat back up to 330°F (166°C) before each set.

DIFFICULTY:

PREP TIME: 30 MINUTES

REST TIME: 1 TO 8 HOURS

COOK TIME: 30 MINUTES

YIELD: 4 SERVINGS

DIETARY NOTES: DAIRY-FREE

KARAAGE

After a long session of karaoke with R. Mika, we swung by a food stall. "How about a little contest, Sakura?" she said, winking, as she ordered enough fried chicken for six people. We had a small crowd cheering us on by the end, and I thought I could keep up with her, but I never stood a chance.

FOR THE WASABI MAYO DIPPING SAUCE:

½ cup (126 g) Japanese mayonnaise

2 to 3 tablespoons (40 to 60 g)
  wasabi, prepared

1 teaspoon (1 g) black pepper

1 tablespoon (18 g) tonkatsu sauce

2 teaspoons (10 ml) rice vinegar

FOR THE KARAAGE:

⅓ cup (79 ml) soy sauce

3 tablespoons (44 ml) sake

8 garlic cloves, grated

1-inch (2.5-cm) piece fresh ginger,
  peeled and grated

1 teaspoon (4 g) sugar

½ teaspoon (1.5 g) salt

1 teaspoon (1 g) black pepper

2 pounds (907 g) boneless, skinless
  chicken thighs, cut into bite-size
  pieces

1 cup (160 g) potato starch

1 teaspoon (2 g) ground ginger

Peanut oil

1 lemon slice

TO MAKE THE DIPPING SAUCE:

Combine all the ingredients in an airtight container. Store in the refrigerator for up to 1 week.

TO MAKE THE KARAAGE:

Combine the soy sauce, sake, garlic, ginger, sugar, salt, and pepper in a large sealable bag. Toss in the chicken thighs and mix together until fully coated. Marinate in the refrigerator for at least 1 hour or up to 8 hours.

After the chicken has marinated, combine the potato starch and ground ginger in a small bowl. Fill a deep heavy pot with 1½ inches of peanut oil, and heat to 325°F (165°C) over medium-high heat.

Transfer the marinated chicken into a large bowl. Drain as much excess liquid as you can, at least to the point that it isn't soaking. Add the potato starch mixture, and mix until all the chicken is covered. It will become pasty and look a bit patchy.

Once the oil has reached the desired temperature, carefully place a few pieces of chicken in the oil, making sure to not overcrowd the pot. Fry for 90 seconds. Transfer to a plate covered with paper towels. Repeat in batches with the remaining chicken.

After all the pieces have been cooked once, increase the oil temperature to 350°F (180°C). Refry all the pieces of chicken in batches for 60 seconds. Transfer to a plate covered with paper towels. The second fry will make the chicken extra crispy! Serve with lemon slices and the dipping sauce on the side.

Sure, American mayo would work fine in this recipe, but I highly recommend that you try and find the Japanese version for this dipping sauce. It makes all the difference!

DIFFICULTY:
PREP TIME: 1 HOUR
REST TIME: 1 HOUR
COOK TIME: 45 MINUTES
YIELD: 6 SERVINGS
DIETARY NOTES: DAIRY-FREE

BEEF MENCHI KATSU

I didn't need to ask Ryu what makes him so strong, because I've been keeping up with him for so long now. At this point, he could turn that question around, because he's what makes me strong. I've wanted to thank him for inspiring me and giving me a dream. I've been meaning to thank him by making one of his favorite things, these amazing beef cutlets. Too bad he never accepts my invitations for dinner.

INGREDIENTS:

3 teaspoons (15 ml) canola oil, divided

½ medium yellow onion, chopped

1 garlic clove, minced

1 pound (454 g) ground beef

3 eggs

1½ cups (100 g) plus 3 tablespoons (14 g) panko bread crumbs, divided

1 tablespoon (19 g) tonkatsu sauce

½ teaspoon (1 g) salt

1¼ teaspoon (1.25 g) black pepper, divided

2 tablespoons (22 g) potato starch

⅓ cup (53 g) all-purpose flour

Peanut oil, for frying

INSTRUCTIONS:

Place a pan over medium-high heat. Add 2 teaspoons of canola oil, onion, and garlic, and cook until softened, about 5 minutes. Remove from the heat and allow to cool completely.

Transfer the onion and garlic into a large bowl. Once completely cooled, add the ground beef, 1 egg, 3 tablespoons of the panko, tonkatsu sauce, salt, and ¼ teaspoon of the black pepper. Mix until well combined.

Divide the meat into 6 equal-size patties. Place on a plate and cover with plastic wrap. Refrigerate for 1 hour.

Prepare 3 bowls for breading. Fill the first bowl with a mixture of potato starch, flour, and the remaining teaspoon (2 g) of black pepper. Whisk the remaining 2 eggs in the second bowl. Fill the last bowl with the remaining 1½ cups (100 g) of panko.

When the patties have finished chilling, pour 2 inches of peanut oil into a deep pot, and heat to 350°F (180°C). Dredge each of the patties first in the potato starch, then the eggs, then the panko. Be sure to coat each patty thoroughly at each stage.

Carefully place the patties into the oil, making sure to not overcrowd the pot. Deep-fry each side for 3 to 4 minutes, or until golden brown. Transfer to a wire rack and let rest for a few minutes before serving.

DIFFICULTY:

PREP TIME: 15 MINUTES

COOK TIME: 30 MINUTES

REST TIME: AT LEAST 2 HOURS

YIELD: 9 SERVINGS

DIETARY NOTES: GLUTEN-FREE, VEGAN

MIZU YOKAN

Ryu is the kind of guy who's always on the move, traveling around the world looking for the next strong opponent to push himself. But any time he's back in Japan, he picks up some mizu yokan to feel like he's home again. Every time I see them, I'm reminded of Ryu and wonder where he's off fighting now.

INGREDIENTS:

1¼ cup (296 ml) water

2 teaspoons (5 g) agar-agar powder

¼ cup (50 g) brown sugar

¼ cup (50 g) sugar

17 ounces (500 g) koshian, also known as red bean paste

Pinch of salt

INSTRUCTIONS:

Whisk together the water and agar-agar in a small saucepan. Place over medium-high heat, and bring to a boil.

Reduce the heat, and add both sugars. Let simmer until the agar-agar and sugars are completely dissolved. Add the koshian and whisk until dissolved.

Add the salt, and whisk in. Remove from the heat then let sit for 2 minutes. Place the saucepan in a bowl of ice water to help cool quicker. Whisk the mixture, and let cool for about 5 minutes.

Pour into an 8½-by-8½-inch (21.5-by-21.5-cm) deep baking pan. Allow the mixture to completely cool. Cover with plastic wrap, and refrigerate for at least 2 hours. Cut into 2-by-2-inch squares. Store in an airtight container in the refrigerator for up to 3 days.

DIFFICULTY: ▬▬ ▬ ▬ ▬

PREP TIME: 20 MINUTES

COOK TIME: 20 MINUTES

REST TIME: 12 HOURS

YIELD: 1 DRINK

DIETARY NOTES: VEGAN

HADOKEN

It took me a long while studying Ryu's moves to figure out how to pull off a Hadoken. Since I was just teaching myself, it was a lot of practice through sweat and tears. At one point, I even tried drinking more blue things to better visualize the attack. I doubt it helped, but I came up with this blue drink to share with Ryu to remind me of the lengths I went to get stronger.

FOR THE YUZU-LEMON SYRUP:

¾ cup (150 g) sugar
½ cup (118 ml) water
¼ cup (59 ml) lemon juice
2 tablespoons (30 ml) lime juice
¼ cup (59 ml) yuzu extract

FOR SERVING:

2½ ounces (74 ml) Yuzu-Lemon
    Syrup
2 ounces (59 ml) shochu
1 ounce (29.5 ml) blue curaçao
Ice
3 ounces (89 ml) club soda

TO MAKE THE YUZU-LEMON SYRUP:

Combine sugar and water in a small saucepan, and place over medium-high heat. Whisk until the sugar dissolves, then bring to a boil. Reduce the heat, and let simmer for 5 minutes. Remove the syrup from the heat, and allow to cool to room temperature.

Combine the syrup, lemon juice, lime juice, and yuzu extract in an airtight container. Cover, and refrigerate for at least 12 hours or up to 2 weeks.

TO SERVE:

Combine the yuzu-lemon syrup, shochu, and curaçao in a cocktail shaker filled with ice. Cover, and shake vigorously for 10 seconds. Strain, and pour into a glass with ice. Fill with club soda.

DIFFICULTY: ━━ ━ ━ ━

PREP TIME: 45 MINUTES

COOK TIME: 15 MINUTES

YIELD: 4 SERVINGS

DIETARY NOTES: DAIRY-FREE

PAD KRA PRAO

I wanted to meet the Fearless Emperor that Dan so often spoke about dethroning, but I was surprised to find a humble Sagat living in a sleepy coastal village in Thailand. When he invited me for some pad kra prao, I told him all the details about his fight with Dan that I've heard over the years. Sagat laughed to himself over a few details Dan almost certainly exaggerated, but he refused to correct the record.

INGREDIENTS:

5 to 8 Thai chiles, stems removed

5 garlic cloves, minced

1½ tablespoons (22 ml) soy sauce

2 teaspoons (10 ml) oyster sauce

2½ teaspoons (12 ml) fish sauce

¼ cup (60 ml) chicken broth

2 teaspoons (8 g) sugar

1 tablespoon (15 ml) canola oil, plus
   more for egg

2 shallots, thinly sliced

1 pound (454 g) boneless, skinless
   chicken breast, finely chopped

1 long bean, cut into bite-size pieces

1¼ cups holy basil leaves

Salt

Black pepper

4 eggs

Canola oil

2 cup (740 g) cooked rice

INSTRUCTIONS:

Place the Thai chiles and garlic cloves in a mortar and pestle. Smash and grind until a paste forms. Combine the soy sauce, oyster sauce, fish sauce, chicken broth, and sugar in a small bowl. Set aside.

Set a wok or large stainless steel pan over high heat. Add a tablespoon of canola oil and then the shallots. Sauté until soft, about 3 minutes. Add the chile-garlic paste, and cook until the garlic starts to turn golden brown.

Add the chicken, and toss until combined with the paste. Add the sauce mixture, and continue to toss until the chicken is almost cooked through. Add the long bean, and mix in well. Continue cooking until the chicken is done. Remove from the heat, and stir in the holy basil. Season with salt and pepper to taste.

In a small saucepan, heat about a quarter inch of canola oil, then add an egg or two directly into the pan, and fry until the edges are browned. Fry the remaining eggs.

To serve, place ½ cup (185 g) rice on a plate, add a spoonful of chicken and top with a fried egg. Repeat with remaining ingredients, and serve.

DIFFICULTY: ━━

PREP TIME: 10 MINUTES

COOK TIME: 30 MINUTES

YIELD: 4 TO 6 DRINKS

DIETARY NOTES: DAIRY, GLUTEN-FREE,
  VEGETARIAN

TIGER SHOT

The night market Sagat and I were conversing in had a drink on the menu called Tiger Shot, named in his honor. I actually noticed a few passersby waving to Sagat and smiling. I love how much appreciation and respect he gets from his compatriots. He said he appreciated the kind words and the drink name, but he still felt remorse for the things in his past.

INGREDIENTS:

6 cups (1420 ml) water
¼ cup (50 g) sugar
6 green cardamom pods, crushed
3 star anise
2 whole cloves
1 cinnamon stick
4 bags Ceylon tea
1 tablespoon (15 ml) vanilla extract
Ice
Orange food dye, optional
2 tablespoons to ¼ cup (30 to 59 ml)
    sweetened condensed milk

INSTRUCTIONS:

Combine the water, sugar, cardamom pods, star anise, cloves, and cinnamon stick in a large pot. Place over medium-high heat, and bring to a boil. Reduce the heat, and simmer for 15 minutes.

Remove from the heat, add the tea bags, cover, and let steep for 10 to 15 minutes. Strain into a large pitcher, and add the vanilla extract. Allow to cool completely, and then place in the refrigerator to chill. Store in the refrigerator for up to 2 weeks.

To serve, prepare a glass with ice. If you are using orange food dye, add one drop over the ice. Fill the glass about three-quarters full with cold tea. Add the sweetened condensed milk, and mix together until well combined.

DIFFICULTY:

PREP TIME: 30 MINUTES

COOK TIME: 10 MINUTES

YIELD: 13 TO 16 RICE BALLS

DIETARY NOTES: VEGAN

RED BEAN ONIGIRI

I just love white rice. I can eat rice with anything, but onigiri is even better than other rice dishes because it's portable. I saw some red bean onigiri at a convenience store and thought it was perfect since it's my favorite food and Ryu's favorite dessert in one package. It's like a Sakura-Ryu tag team punch for your taste buds! Oh, please don't tell Ryu I said that, he'd never let it go.

INGREDIENTS:

One 16-ounce (430 g) can sweetened red beans, mashed
3 cups cooked Sushi Rice (page 27)
Furikake (optional)

INSTRUCTIONS:

In a large bowl, mix the mashed red beans with the rice. Prepare a small bowl of water to keep your hands moist during the process. Wet your hands, and take a handful of the bean-rice mixture and form triangle shapes. Use a moderate amount of pressure so the onigiri holds its shape. To add a slightly savory flavor to these, dip the edge in a bit of furikake.

Until ready to serve, wrap each onigiri in plastic, and store in the refrigerator for up to 1 week.

DIFFICULTY:

PREP TIME: 30 MINUTES

COOK TIME: 20 MINUTES

YIELD: 13 TO 16 RICE BALLS

DIETARY NOTES: DAIRY-FREE

SALMON ONIGIRI

There's a super cute onigiri stall on my way to work that sells amazing salmon onigiri. I like to buy two each time I walk by: one for the walk and one for when I'm on break. It's a nice motivator to get through a workday. On a good day, I'll happily buy two more on the way home to enjoy. But on a difficult day, if some jerk breaks one of the claw machines, I tend to buy three or four. Look, they are really good, okay?

INGREDIENTS:

1 pound (454 g) salmon, cut into
  4 pieces

Salt

Black pepper

2 tablespoons (15 ml) soy sauce

4 scallions, chopped

3 cups cooked Sushi Rice (page 27),
  room temperature

Nori (optional)

INSTRUCTIONS:

Place a pan over medium-high heat. Generously salt and pepper the salmon. Place the salmon skin-side down on the pan. Cook until the skin crisps up, about 4 minutes. Flip the salmon over, and cook for another 2 minutes.

Remove the salmon from the pan, separate from the skin, and break into pieces. Return the flaked salmon to the pan, and add the soy sauce. Cook until the salmon has absorbed the soy sauce, about 2 minutes.

Place the salmon on a plate, and add the scallions. Mix the salmon with the rice. Wet your hands, take a handful of the rice, and form triangle shapes. Use a moderate amount of pressure so the onigiri holds its shape. Lightly wet the edges of a small nori piece and place on the bottom, wrapping around the onigiri. Until ready to serve, wrap each onigiri in plastic, and store in the refrigerator for up to 1 week.

DIFFICULTY:

PREP TIME: 20 MINUTES

COOK TIME: 20 MINUTES

YIELD: 4 SERVINGS

DIETARY NOTES: DAIRY-FREE

OYAKODON

A few years ago when I went looking for Ryu, I embarked on a boat with Dan and Blanka. I was training up and down the deck every day, doing everything I could to get trained and ready. I even cooked for the whole crew! But It's hard making food for that many people, so I relied on my tried-and-true oyakodon. It's full of protein to get you up on your feet and training again, and it tastes great to boot!

INGREDIENTS:

½ cup (118 ml) dashi stock

2 tablespoons (59 ml) soy sauce

1 tablespoon (30 ml) mirin

1 tablespoon (30 ml) sake

4 teaspoons (8 g) sugar, divided

2 teaspoons (10 ml) canola oil

1½ medium yellow onions, diced

1½ pounds (680 g) boneless,
  skinless chicken thighs, diced

2 scallions, diced, plus more for
  serving

Salt

Black pepper

4 eggs

2 cups (740 g) white rice, cooked

Shredded nori, for serving

Ichimi togarashi, for serving

INSTRUCTIONS:

Combine the dashi stock, soy sauce, mirin, sake, and 2 teaspoons sugar in a small bowl, and set aside.

Place a medium-size pan over medium-high heat, and add the canola oil. Add the onions, and cook until softened, about 8 minutes.

Add the dashi mixture to the pan, and bring to a boil. Add the chicken, and reduce the heat to a simmer. Cook until the chicken is just about done, 6 to 8 minutes. Reduce the heat to low. Add half the scallions, and season with salt, pepper, and the remaining sugar. Set aside.

In a medium bowl, scramble the eggs, and carefully stream them into the pan, making sure the egg is evenly distributed. Cover, and cook until the eggs are just set but still slightly runny. Portion out ½ cup of cooked rice into four bowls, then spoon the chicken mixture over the rice, top with additional scallions, nori, and ichimi togarashi, and serve.

DIFFICULTY: ▬▬▬▬ ▬ ▬

PREP TIME: 1 HOUR

COOK TIME: 15 MINUTES

YIELD: 8 SKEWERS

DIETARY NOTES: DAIRY-FREE

CURRY FISH BALLS

I wanted to ask Yang on his work break all about how he and his brother train together and manage to support each other so well, but I got a little sidetracked asking about hair-care tips. Yang's hairstyle is just so distracting that we went down a long road of hair products and routines. Before I knew it, I had finished an entire plate of curry fish balls without asking a single thing about fighting, and Yang had to get back to the customers.

FOR THE CURRY PASTE:

2 shallots, chopped

3 garlic cloves

2-inch (5-cm) piece fresh ginger, peeled and sliced

1 lemongrass stalk, chopped

¼ cup fresh cilantro

3 small dried red chiles

1 tablespoon (8 g) ground coriander

2 teaspoons (4 g) ground turmeric

1 teaspoon (3 g) ground cumin

1 tablespoon (15 ml) fish sauce

½ teaspoon black pepper

Juice and zest of 1 lime

FOR THE CURRY:

Canola oil, for pan

2 shallots, chopped

3 garlic cloves, chopped

3 tablespoons (30 g) all-purpose flour

½ cup Curry Paste

1 cup (237 ml) fish stock

1 cup (237 ml) coconut milk

1 tablespoon (19 g) palm sugar

24 fish balls

TO MAKE THE CURRY PASTE:

In a food processor, place all the ingredients, and pulse until it resembles a thick salsa. Store in the refrigerator for up to 1 week.

TO MAKE THE CURRY:

Place a frying pan over medium-high heat with canola oil. Add the shallots, and cook until softened, about 5 minutes. Add the garlic, and cook for another 2 minutes.

Add the flour and curry paste. After the flour and curry have combined with the shallots and garlic, slowly add the stock, coconut milk, and palm sugar while whisking. Finally, add the fish balls.

Bring to a boil, and reduce the heat to a simmer for 10 minutes or until the fish balls have heated through. If serving these with a skewer, carefully skewer 3 fish balls per skewer.

! **Feel free to use a premade curry paste if you can't find all the ingredients!**

! **Fish balls can be found in most Asian grocery stores in a variety of shapes, both frozen and fresh.**

197

DIFFICULTY: ▬ ▬ ▬ ▬ ▬

PREP TIME: 1 HOUR

REST TIME: 2½ HOURS

COOK TIME: 30 MINUTES

YIELD: 16 BAO

DIETARY NOTES: DAIRY-FREE

CHICKEN BAOZI

When I visited Yun's food stall, I asked to see his best version of the restaurant's namesake, the Shoryuken, but he confessed he didn't know how. I was happy to try to teach him my version, but I don't think he quite got the hang of it. We did manage to work up a huge hunger and demolished an order of Yun's favorite, chicken baozi.

FOR THE DOUGH:

1½ teaspoons (5 g) active dry yeast

¾ cup (177 ml) warm water

¼ cup (59 ml) canola oil, plus more
    for bowl

2¼ cups (326 g) all-purpose flour,
    plus more for work surface

¾ cup (108 g) cornstarch

2 teaspoons (10 g) baking powder

2 teaspoons (8 g) fennel seed,
    ground

¼ cup (50 g) sugar

2 teaspoons (6 g) salt

FOR THE FILLING:

1½ pounds (680 g) ground chicken

5 scallions, finely chopped

6 shiitake mushrooms, finely
    chopped

2-inch (5-cm) piece fresh ginger,
    peeled and grated

2 garlic cloves, minced

1 tablespoon (15 ml) soy sauce

2 tablespoons (30 ml) Shaoxing wine

1 teaspoon (5 ml) sesame oil

2 teaspoons (8 g) sugar

1 teaspoon (3 g) salt

2 teaspoons (3 g) black pepper

1 tablespoon (9 g) cornstarch

FOR FRYING:

1 tablespoon (15 ml) canola oil

¼ cup (59 ml) water

TO MAKE THE DOUGH:

Mix the yeast, water, and canola oil in a small bowl, and let rest for 5 minutes, allowing the yeast to become active and frothy.

Combine the flour, cornstarch, baking powder, fennel seed, sugar, and salt in a large bowl. Slowly mix in the liquid until the dough comes together. Transfer dough to a lightly floured work surface, and knead for 5 minutes. Place the dough in an oiled bowl, and cover. Let it rest at room temperature until it doubles in size, about 2 hours.

TO MAKE THE FILLING:

Combine all the ingredients in a bowl until just mixed without overworking it. Divide into 16 equal portions. The filling might be a bit loose, but try to form into round portions. Freeze for at least 20 minutes or until ready to form the bao. This will make the bao easier to seal.

TO ASSEMBLE:

Punch down the dough, and roll it out into a long tube. Divide into 16 equal pieces, and form into balls. Take a portion, and roll it out to about 5 inches wide. When rolling, make sure the center isn't too thin. Add 1 of the filling portions in the center. Pleat the buns until sealed. Repeat with the remaining portions.

Place a large pan over medium-high heat with canola oil. Add the bao to the pan, making sure to give each a half inch of space around itself. Pan-fry the bao until the bottoms turn golden brown.

Add water to the pan. Cover, and let steam for 5 minutes or until the water has evaporated completely.

Cook for an additional 30 seconds to 1 minute to fully crisp up the bottoms.

DIFFICULTY: ▬▬▬▬▭▬▭▬▭▬ ▬▬

PREP TIME: 30 MINUTES

REST TIME: 2 HOURS

COOK TIME: 15 MINUTES

YIELD: 13 PANCAKES

DIETARY NOTES: DAIRY-FREE, PORK

HIROSHIMA-STYLE OKONOMIYAKI

I've wanted to ask Zeku for a while now how he changes his age mid-fight. Oh, but don't get me wrong, I don't want to look younger or anything. I just think I could learn from strength like that. I asked him, and he took me to an okonomiyaki shop. He rambled a bit about Bushinryu and his ninja training, but I don't think I understood much of it. I was halfway through my meal when he abruptly stood up, thanked me for the meal, changed appearances, and walked right out without paying! That jerk! How did he finish before me?

FOR THE BATTER:

2 teaspoons (3 g) bonito flakes, finely ground

1 cup (155 g) cake flour

½ teaspoon (2 g) baking powder

1 cup (237 ml) water

Cooking spray

4 Napa cabbage leaves, thinly sliced

2 scallions, thinly sliced

½ cup bean sprouts

¼ cup crushed potato chips, plus more for topping

15 thin slices pork belly

3 packages yakisoba noodles

3 teaspoons sake, divided

Okonomiyaki sauce, store bought

3 eggs

Japanese mayonnaise, for topping

Aonori flakes, for topping

Chopped scallions, for topping

INSTRUCTIONS:

Combine the ground bonito flakes, cake flour, and baking powder in a small bowl. Whisk in the water until smooth. Cover, and refrigerate for 2 hours.

Place a griddle over medium heat. Once heated, coat the pan with cooking spray. Ladle ⅓ cup (79 ml) of the batter, and spread it out to 8 inches (20 cm), round and thin.

Top with Napa cabbage, scallions, bean sprouts, and potato chips. Place 4 to 5 slices of pork belly on top. Pour about 1 tablespoon (15 ml) of batter across the pork belly.

Using 2 spatulas, carefully but quickly flip the entire pancake so the pork belly is on the bottom. Carefully push this to the side, and make sure everything stays together between the pancake and the pork belly.

Increase the heat to medium-high. Take a package of yakisoba noodles and separate them. Place on the griddle, and add a teaspoon of sake. Stir-fry the noodles until warm. Add 1 to 3 tablespoons of okonomiyaki sauce. Toss until all the noodles are coated. Carefully shape into a circle similar in size to the okonomiyaki. Transfer the okonomiyaki and noodles on top of the noodles.

Add more cooking spray, and place an egg on the griddle. Quickly spread the egg to match the circular shape and size of the okonomiyaki. Once spread, while the egg is still runny, transfer the okonomiyaki and noodles on top. Cook for about 30 seconds.

Place a plate on top of the okonomiyaki and flip it over, putting the egg on top. Repeat the process to make two additional okonomiyaki. Generously cover the okonomiyaki with okonomiyaki sauce, Japanese mayo, aonori, scallions, and potato chips, then serve.

(!) Typically okonomiyaki uses tenkasu (bits of deep-fried batter) to add a little crunch, but Zeku insisted I substitute it with potato chips.

INDEX

INDEX

ABOUT THE AUTHOR

Victoria Rosenthal launched her blog, Pixelated Provisions, in 2012 to combine her lifelong passions for video games and food by recreating consumables found in many of her favorite games. When she isn't experimenting in the kitchen and dreaming up new recipes, she spends her days developing graphics for NASA. She resides in Houston, Texas, with her husband and corgi. Victoria is also the author of *Fallout: The Vault Dweller's Official Cookbook* and *Destiny: The Official Cookbook*.

ACKNOWLEDGMENTS

Thanks to Jeff Rosenthal, Kanji, Kate McKean, Matt Thomas, Keenan Maistry, Casey Gordon, and Rene Rodriguez for the hyper armor. Huge shout-outs to Kevin Stich, Irvin Chavira, Harry Readinger, Nina Freeman, Elaine Gray, Heather Winter, Richard Poskozim, Nick Esparza, Forrest Porter, Rebekah Valentine, Saam Pahlavan, Brock Wright, my family, and the Pixelated Provisions' community for all their help with the neutral game.

INSIGHT EDITIONS

PO Box 3088
San Rafael, CA 94912
www.insighteditions.com

f Find us on Facebook: www.facebook.com/InsightEditions
🐦 Follow us on Twitter: @insighteditions

Library of Congress Cataloging-in-Publication Data available.

ISBN: 978-1-64722-168-3

Publisher: Raoul Goff
VP of Licensing: Vanessa Lopez
VP of Creative: Chrissy Kwasnik
VP of Manufacturing: Alix Nicholaeff
Designer: Monique Narboneta
Senior Editor: Amanda Ng
Associate Editor: Maya Alpert
Managing Editor: Lauren LePera
Production Editor: Jennifer Bentham
Senior Production Manager: Greg Steffen
Senior Production Manager, Subsidiary Rights: Lina s Palma

ROOTS of PEACE 🍁 REPLANTED PAPER

Insight Editions, in association with Roots of Peace, will plant two trees for each tree used in the manufacturing of this book. Roots of Peace is an internationally renowned humanitarian organization dedicated to eradicating land mines worldwide and converting war-torn lands into productive farms and wildlife habitats. Roots of Peace will plant two million fruit and nut trees in Afghanistan and provide farmers there with the skills and support necessary for sustainable land use.

Manufactured in China by Insight Editions

10 9 8 7 6 5 4 3 2 1